Vision and Transformation

For thirty years Sangharakshita has been playing an important part in the spread of
Buddhism throughout the modern world. He is head of the Western Buddhist Order
(Trailokya Bauddha Mahasangha), and is actively engaged in what is now an
international Buddhist movement with centres in thirteen countries worldwide. When
not visiting centres he is based at a community in Norfolk. His writings are available in
eleven languages.

Also by Sangharakshita:
Messengers from Tibet and Other Poems
A Survey of Buddhism
Flame in Darkness
The Enchanted Heart
The Three Jewels
The Essence of Zen
Crossing the Stream
The Path of the Inner Life
The Thousand-Petalled Lotus
Human Enlightenment
The Religion of Art
The Ten Pillars of Buddhism
The Eternal Legacy
Travel Letters
Alternative Traditions
Conquering New Worlds
Ambedkar and Buddhism
The History of My Going for Refuge
The Taste of Freedom
New Currents in Western Buddhism
A Guide to the Buddhist Path
Learning to Walk

The Meaning of Orthodoxy in Buddhism
Mind—Reactive and Creative
Aspects of Buddhist Morality
Buddhism and Blasphemy
Buddhism, World Peace, and Nuclear War
The Bodhisattva: Evolution and Self-Transcendence
The Glory of the Literary World
Going For Refuge
The Caves of Bhaja
My Relation to the Order
Hercules and the Birds and Other Poems

Vision and Transformation:
An Introduction to the Buddha's
Noble Eightfold Path

Sangharakshita

Windhorse Publications

Published by Windhorse Publications
Unit 1-316 The Custard Factory
Gibb Street, Birmingham, B9 4AA

First published 1990
Reprinted 1995

Cover design Dhammarati

Printed by Redwood Books,
Trowbridge, Wiltshire

British Library Cataloguing in Publication Data
Sangharakshita, *Bhikshu, Sthavira, 1925—*
Vision and Transformation.
1. Buddhism
Rn : Dennis P. E. Lingwood   I. Title
294.3
ISBN 0-904766-44-6

Table of Contents

Introduction

'It is excellent, Bhante! Excellent! It is as though one had set upright what had been upset, or disclosed what had been covered, or shown the way to one who was lost, or brought a lamp into the darkness so that those with eyes might see.'

These words were originally addressed to the Buddha about five hundred years before the birth of Jesus, but they quite accurately describe my own feelings when—some two-and-a-half-thousand years later—I first came across the core of the teachings set out in this book. I first read the edited transcripts of the talks collected in this volume in the magazine *Mitrata*. I expected at best to come away from the experience a little better informed. I did not really expect to be interested. Like most Buddhists I knew that the Eightfold Path was supposed to be central to the Buddha's teachings, and I felt I should make an effort to know more about it. But what I had heard did not fill me with enthusiasm. The dry list—'right' this and 'right' that —sounded dull, dusty, platitudinous. Hardly the sort of stuff to open up new horizons. In fact, to be honest, a bore.

But in the event these lectures turned out to be anything *but* a bore, and the reason for this is clearly brought out in the title chosen for this volume—*Vision and Transformation*. As I read the transcripts of these talks I found that I was being told that my concept of the aim of Buddhism—and, it seemed, the concept of many other Western Buddhists as well—was seriously one-sided. I was being told that vision—knowing, understanding, even insight, even those clear experiences I was so attached to—that none of this was enough. None of this was the goal of the Buddhist path. It was just the beginning.

What Sangharakshita was telling me was that these initial glimpses of the light are merely invitations—or challenges—to a deep and difficult process of transformation. He was telling me—what I already secretly knew—that the dead weight of my habits, conditioning, and instincts meant that my centre of gravity was not going to be shifted by any mere insight. What was required was more like an earthquake. To shift this weight I would have to work not just on my head but on my heart, not just on my heart but on my belly, and not just on myself but on my whole world. To do this I would need to want this transformation as much as I had ever wanted anything— as much as I had wanted money, or success, or a woman. To use more genteel and abstract language, I would need to 'engage my emotions'.

At another time I would probably have chosen to ignore this unwelcome message, and simply looked for a more congenial teacher. But far from being disappointed, I was delighted. It was as though a very solid and obvious brick wall had been pointed out to me—a wall which had been blocking my path, and which I had been trying to walk through as though it was not there. Once seen this wall was so large and self-evident I could hardly believe it had escaped my attention for so long. Of course I would have to walk around it. And, true, the way ahead now looked much longer and more difficult. But at least there *was* a way ahead.

What I have described are my own personal reactions to the talks recorded in this book, and if they were purely

personal they would not be of much interest or importance. But I believe the problems I was experiencing are
common. I believe—and I have seen and heard much
evidence to support my belief—that because of some
prevalent misconceptions about the nature of human
beings and spiritual growth, there are many other people
who are also trying to walk through this same invisible
brick wall.

The misconceptions that lead us to try to walk through
this wall arise because we identify ourselves almost completely with the surface, conscious levels of our minds, and
we ignore our depths. We overestimate the power of
reason and intellect, and forget that our real motivations
come from far deeper springs—from emotion, instinct,
myth. Because of this superficial view of ourselves we are
not only unaware of the real forces that drive us, we are
not even aware that we are unaware.

When applied to the spiritual life these attitudes have
some predictable consequences. The most obvious is that
we think that to know and understand is enough. We think
that when our conscious outlook changes, *we* have
changed. We think that vision is all-important, and we
forget about the need for transformation. Then, as our
vision grows, we come to feel more and more deeply
dissatisfied, because the other changes we expect to see in
our lives do not follow. The patterns of our everyday
feeling and behaviour seem stuck in the same dismal old
channels. And although we are definitely looking at the
stars—to turn Oscar Wilde's famous words on their head
—we still seem to be lying in the gutter.

This conflict between our conscious views and our
deeper volitions means that we make little progress. Consciously we may think we are completely committed to
spiritual growth. But what our untransformed depths
seem to want from life are still money, recognition,

security, sex, food, family, and so on—the list will vary a little from person to person. So perhaps we try to fool ourselves, making our spiritual life into a pleasant little hobby, making our meditation an escape, and meanwhile turning a blind eye to the fact that our lives and ruling passions are hardly different from those of our materialist neighbours. Alternatively we may seek to override our real drives, trying to live up to our ideals by sheer strength of will—and then we wonder why we feel deeply divided and unhappy. Or perhaps we swerve wildly from one extreme to the other, alternating periods of wilful effort with spells of unreconstructed hedonism.

The teachings Sangharakshita presents in this book offer a way out of this impasse. They do this by showing that the Buddhist path is a process of organic growth, through which spiritual vision is not only encouraged for its own sake, but is also made to catalyse the transformation of *all* aspects of our being, low as well as high, unconscious as well as conscious. By this process even our murkiest depths are exposed to the transforming light of our vision, so that they can help—rather than block—our efforts to grow. The goal of the Buddhist Path is presented as not just insight—at least not in any sense in which we are likely to understand the word—but as the growth of our total being. Our being is compared to a young tree, and our spiritual vision to the rain which nourishes it, and which encourages it to put out first leaves and then flowers. Perhaps the rain falls on everyone. But only a few have the energy and courage to fully co-operate with the growth it promotes.

In the talks recorded in this book Sangharakshita reveals a depth of significance and relevance in the teaching of the Noble Eightfold Path that few people will probably have suspected it contained. In the process he presents an enormous amount of doctrine. Most of this is highly traditional Buddhist doctrine, presented in a highly traditional Buddhist way—as list upon list, and list within list. Here we have not only the Eightfold Path itself, but also the Four Noble Truths, the Three Characteristics of Conditioned Existence, the Four *Śūnyatās*, the Four 'Sublime Abodes', the Five *Śīlas* and the Five Dharmas, the Four Exertions, the Five Hindrances, the Four (or Eight) *Dhyānas*, and more. This might not sound an attractive prospect. The age-old Buddhist habit of list-making is not to everybody's taste, and readers might be excused for expecting these lists to turn the Dharma into something drab and dead. But in Sangharakshita's hands the opposite seems to happen. The lists come alive, and what seemed at first a rather dowdy collection of heirlooms are dusted off, given a polish and shine, and placed at just the right angle to the light to show off their full lustre, their full relevance to the spiritual strivings of men and women in the late twentieth century.

As well as a wealth of traditional Buddhist doctrine these pages also contain ideas and formulations which may not be familiar to Buddhists from outside the Friends of the Western Buddhist Order (FWBO). Some of these, like the rearrangement of the traditional *foundations of mindfulness* into four rather different *levels of awareness*, merely represent a shuffling and a simplification of traditional material. Others, like the concept of 'The Higher Evolution'—presenting the development of consciousness as the underlying significance of the evolutionary process, and Buddhahood as its final goal—are more uniquely Sangharakshita's.

Buddhists from outside the FWBO are often suspicious of some of Sangharakshita's apparently more personal interpretations of the Dharma. They are right to be so—Sangharakshita himself is at pains to point out that originality is not a virtue in a Buddhist teacher. But it would be a shame if this suspicion were allowed to obscure the value Sangharakshita's teachings could have for all Buddhists, and especially for Buddhists in the West. Some of his interpretations of the Dharma are radical, but they are radical only in the best sense. The word radical comes from the Latin for 'root', and it means deriving from the root, the basis, the foundation. Sangharakshita's teachings do indeed derive from the very roots of Buddhism, and they attempt to express its basic message in a way which is relevant to our present circumstances. Sometimes his ideas seem radical because they are in fact more genuinely traditional, and derive from older sources, than the teachings of some surviving Asian Buddhist schools.

Among the most radical of Sangharakshita's teachings are those concerned with work and livelihood. Newcomers to Sangharakshita, hearing his comments on this subject, especially from the earlier days of the FWBO, are often impressed by his vigorous blasphemy against the conventional work ethic. And in the talk on Right Livelihood recorded here, Sangharakshita *could* seem—Heaven forbid!—to be advising most of his listeners to do as little work as they can get away with.

However a few comments are needed to put this advice into context. Sangharakshita delivered this series of lectures in 1968, shortly after the founding of the FWBO, and before the ordination of the first members of the Western Buddhist Order. In the decades since 1968 the FWBO has grown into a worldwide movement, and members of this movement have put a great deal of energy into setting up and running what are called—rather inelegantly—'team-based Right Livelihood businesses'. These not only provide Buddhists with the opportunity to earn an ethical livelihood in co-operation with like-minded people, at their best they can transform work from pointless drudgery into a spiritual practice.

The history of team-based Right Livelihood businesses has admittedly been mixed. Over the years there have been successes, and there have been failures—financial and otherwise. But most important this experiment in Right Livelihood has provided an opportunity to learn from both success *and* failure. No doubt if he were writing on this subject today Sangharakshita would draw heavily on this fund of experience. No doubt also his emphasis would be different from what it was in 1968, when for most Buddhists work meant a meaningless job one was forced to do to pay the bills.

Today there are many more opportunities for Buddhists in the FWBO—even those not fortunate enough to be nurses, doctors, teachers, creative artists, and so on—to make their work something approaching what Sangharakshita in this book calls *vocation*. Work becomes vocation when it is directly related to what is most meaningful in the life of the individual. For those for whom Buddhism is the most meaningful part of life, working in a Buddhist team-based business—and helping to transform society in the process—can be a true vocation. The experience of the last few decades indicates that it can also be a powerful tool for personal growth.

Co-operative work seen as a spiritual practice has become one of the distinctive features of the FWBO. In another context Sangharakshita has called work 'the tantric guru'. A tantric guru is a teacher who sees through our self-deceptions, and reflects our true face back at us. He shows us the faults we must overcome, and the challenges we are avoiding. He shows us where to find our full strength, courage, and energy. Work can be our tantric guru because it too is a mirror that shows us our true face, revealing not only our weaknesses but also the unsuspected depths of our strength. Only when we join in the rough and tumble of working with other people do we see how far—or how little—we have really progressed. Only when we challenge our fears and weaknesses in the unforgiving arena of the material world can we genuinely grow out of them. Only when we extend our energies do we find out how potent we really are.

This is not the place for a full discussion of Right Livelihood and the FWBO, but a few words on the subject are needed to bring readers up to date with Sangharakshita's present thinking on the subject, informed as this is by more than twenty years of practical experience gained since these talks were given. This experience has not invalidated what Sangharakshita says about Right Livelihood in this book. But it has certainly added to it.

So much has happened since these talks were delivered —in the FWBO, in the Buddhist scene, and in society and the world in general—that it is not surprising that I should have to say a few words to point out where altered circumstances might call for a change in approach or emphasis. What *is* surprising is that I should have to say so little. But because of the back-to-basics quality that characterizes Sangharakshita's teaching, these talks will not date quickly. Personally I am grateful to have come across them, and to have had the opportunity to study them, both as tape recordings and as edited transcripts in *Mitrata* magazine. I am also grateful to have had the opportunity make them available to a wider, non-FWBO audience, by re-editing them and preparing them for publication in book form. I hope others find them as useful as I have.

Chris Pauling
Vimalakula Community
October 1990

I *The Nature of Existence*
Perfect Vision

However little we may know about Buddhism we will at least know that it is a Path or Way. It is a Path or Way leading to a state of realization of Truth, or of oneness with Reality, which we call Enlightenment, or Nirvana, or the realization of one's own innate Buddhahood. This Path or Way finds expression in a number of different formulations, and of these the Noble Eightfold Path is probably the best known.

The Noble Eightfold Path is the fourth of the Four Noble Truths. If we turn to the Buddha's First Discourse, the Discourse on the Turning the Wheel of the Dharma, which he delivered in the Deer Park at Sarnath shortly after his attainment of Supreme Enlightenment, we find that the principal contents of this Discourse, in which the Buddha communicated his great spiritual discovery to humanity, were the Four Noble Truths: suffering, the cause of suffering, the cessation of suffering, and the way leading to the cessation of suffering—the last of these being none other than the Noble Eightfold Path.

Moreover if we follow the course of Buddhist history, then in school after school, tradition after tradition, whether in India, Tibet, Burma, Thailand, Japan, or Ceylon, wherever Buddhism has spread, we find reference is again and again made to the Four Noble Truths, and especially to the Noble Eightfold Path. Therefore un-

less we know about these Truths, and especially the Truth
of the path—unless we understand them in some detail—
we know very little about Buddhism.

The term Noble Eightfold Path is a translation of the
Sanskrit *ārya-aṣṭāṅgika-mārga* (Pali *ariya-aṭṭhāṅgika-magga*),
the word which we render in English as 'noble' being *ārya*.
In India in ancient times this word was originally used in
a more or less racial sense, designating the invaders who
poured down into the plains of India from central Asia
through the passes of the north-west, conquering the in-
digenous people. Gradually as the centuries went by the
term *ārya* and its related form 'aryan' assumed an ethical
and spiritual meaning. In Buddhism the word connotes
whatever pertains either directly or indirectly to the
realization of Ultimate Reality. Whatever is concerned
with things spiritual, be it the spiritual path itself, or the
spiritual goal, or any aspect of the spiritual life, can be
designated *ārya*. Thus *ārya* means not only 'noble' but also
'holy'.

Some translators therefore speak not only of the Four
Noble Truths and the Noble Eightfold Path, but of the Four
Holy Truths and the *Holy* Eightfold Path. (Lama Govinda
once told me an amusing story. In the early days of Buddhism in Germany there were two rival groups, one insisting
that *ārya* meant 'noble', the other that it meant 'holy'. These
two groups, the Noble Truthers and the Holy Truthers,
were always at loggerheads. Besides illustrating the way
in which people fall out, this story underscores the point
that one should not allow oneself to be carried away by
words. Though admittedly there is some difference between 'noble' and 'holy', the whole controversy was about
a matter of comparatively minor importance.)

The Sanskrit word *aṣṭa* means simply 'eight', while *aṅga*
means 'limb', 'member', or even 'shoot'. In some modern
Indian languages, for instance, one speaks of *pañcāṅga-*

praṇāma or prostration with the 'five limbs', that is to say the two arms, the two legs, and the head. (In Sanskrit and Pali the head is called the *uttamāṅga* or 'highest member'.) Thus although we usually think of the Noble Eightfold Path as consisting of eight successive steps or stages, the use of the word *aṅga* suggests that the steps are not so much successive as simultaneous. In reality the path is eightfold in the sense of being eight-limbed or eight-membered, rather than of being made up of eight steps. *Mārga* means 'path' or 'way'.

Perfect Vision

The first so-called step of the Noble Eightfold Path is called *samyag-dṛṣṭi* in Sanskrit (*sammā-diṭṭhi* in Pali). This is usually translated as Right Understanding, but such a rendition is far from satisfactory. Here, as is so often the case with Buddhist terms and expressions, we can get at the real meaning of the words only by going back to the original language. What then does *samyag-dṛṣṭi* really mean? *Samyak* (or *samyag*), which is prefixed to all eight *aṅgas* or limbs of the Path, means 'proper', 'whole', 'thorough', 'integral', 'complete', 'perfect'. It is certainly not 'right' as opposed to 'wrong'. If one speaks of 'Right Understanding' one gives the impression of a 'right' understanding as opposed to a 'wrong' understanding, or 'right' action as opposed to 'wrong' action, and so on. One gives the impression of a rather narrow, purely moralistic interpretation of the Path. But *samyak* means much more than just 'right'. As I have said, it is also 'whole', 'integral', 'complete', 'perfect'. Probably 'perfect' is the best translation.

Dṛṣṭi is from a root meaning 'to see', and it means 'sight', 'view', 'vision'. It is not just 'understanding', and certainly not understanding in the purely theoretical, intellectual, or abstract sense. It is something direct, immediate, and intuitive. If we unthinkingly translate *samyag-dṛṣṭi*, the first step of the Path, as 'Right Understanding', a subtle misconception is introduced at the very outset of our study—and our practice—of the Buddha's teaching. *Samyag-dṛṣṭi* is much more like 'Integral View' or 'Perfect Vision'. Translating in this way we get much closer to the real meaning, closer to the inner feel of the expression. If you compare the two translations, trying to savour their spiritual quality, you will find that 'Perfect Vision' conveys something different from 'Right Understanding'. 'Right Understanding' is rather trite, rather ordinary, rather intellectual. But if you say 'Perfect Vision' it is as though a whole new world has opened up, as though an extra dimension had been introduced. Let it therefore be 'Perfect Vision': a vision, speaking provisionally, of the nature of existence, of the truth or reality of things.

The Path of Vision and the Path of Transformation
According to the Indian Buddhist tradition the Noble Eightfold Path falls quite naturally into two great divisions. The first of these is known as the Path of Vision (*darśana-mārga*), the second as the Path of Transformation (*bhāvanā-mārga*). Thus the Noble Eightfold Path comprises two lesser 'Paths', in the sense of two successive stages. The Path of Vision corresponds only to the first *aṅga*, or so-called step, Perfect Vision. The Path of Transformation corresponds to the seven remaining 'steps': Perfect Emotion, Perfect Speech, Perfect Action, Perfect Livelihood, Perfect Effort, Perfect Awareness, and Perfect Meditation. The significance of this division is that Perfect Vision represents the phase of initial spiritual insight and experience, whereas the rest of the Eightfold Path represents the transformation of one's whole being, in all its heights and depths, in all its aspects, in accordance with that initial insight and experience. The Path of Transformation repre-

sents a complete and thoroughgoing transformation of one's emotional life, speech, communication with others, livelihood, and so on. One may transform one's livelihood, which is the fifth 'step', before one's speech, which is only the third; but eventually, in one way or another, the whole being is to be transformed, in its heights and in its depths, conscious and unconscious.

Now this initial spiritual experience—this Perfect Vision or Path of Vision—may arise in different ways for different people. There is no uniform pattern. Indeed the great variety that exists among people also shows itself in the spiritual life generally, and in the way people enter upon the spiritual path.

For some people the Path of Vision arises as the result of personal tragedy, bereavement, or loss. Their whole existence is disturbed and upset as though by a great earthquake in which everything they had cherished or held dear is laid low. In this wreck, this ruin of their lives, they start questioning, start looking deeper, start wondering about the meaning and purpose of existence.

For others Perfect Vision may arise by way of a spontaneous mystical experience. (I don't like this word 'mystical', which for many people is redolent of mystery and mystery-mongering. But we don't have a better one.) One can find a number of such mystical experiences described in Bucke's *Cosmic Consciousness*, a book published in 1901 which is still worth reading. It is surprising how many people have had an experience of this kind, some rare moment of ecstacy, or insight, or tremendous love, which apparently without any preparation possessed them, swept them away, lifted them up into a new dimension, and completely altered their outlook on life. Also under the heading of mystical experience we can include our experience of nature, as when we are overwhelmed by the sight of some wonderful sunset, or when in the midst of the countryside we experience a great, all-pervading peace, stillness, and tranquillity.

Sometimes the Path of Vision can arise as a result of looking at a beautiful painting, or listening to music. On such occasions we can be carried away into a new dimension of existence. Sometimes it can arise as a result of deep and prolonged thought. Some people endeavour to reach out and grasp the truth by means of the intellect. They try to plumb the depths of being with reason and logic. This is the way of the thinker, the philosopher, the sage. Some people actually *think* their way through to Reality, to the Path of Vision.

For others it may arise in quite a different way, as the result of the practice of meditation. When the mind has been systematically stilled, and when, although thoughts have been banished clear consciousness still persists, then under these conditions also Perfect Vision may arise.

Sometimes it may arise for those who are engaged in altruistic activities, such as nursing the sick and looking after the old. For those who are sacrificing themselves and their personal interests, and who are completely selfless on the plane of work and action, even in the midst of their activity Perfect Vision may arise.

Finally it may arise, for some people at least, out of their whole experience of life—especially as they grow older, and it is to be hoped more mature. When all the different threads seemingly come together, and the pattern of their lives seems to make some kind of sense, to reflect some glimmer of meaning, then out of the depths of their simple human maturity Perfect Vision may arise. I am not suggesting that wisdom comes automatically with age. Far from it! If such were the case we need not take the trouble to acquire wisdom when young. But certainly for those who have led a truly human life, as they mellow and perhaps sweeten a little, and as their experience clarifies, the Path of Vision may sometimes arise.

Thus the Path of Vision may arise for different people in all these different ways. For some it has even arisen in a dream. But however it does arise we should be very careful not to lose it, not to forget it. This happens very easily, for as the poet says, 'the world is too much with us.' We may have an experience so wonderful that we might think we will never forget it. But after a short time, after a few days or weeks, it is no longer there. It is as though it had never been. So we should cherish it, cultivate it, dwell upon it—try to deepen it, clarify it, develop it—all the time. We should eventually try to allow it to permeate and transform our whole being, our whole life.

To sum up we may say that the aim of this great Buddhist teaching of the Path of Vision and the Path of Transformation is to enable us to bring the whole of our life up to the level of its highest moments. This is what it means to evolve spiritually. This is what it means to follow the Noble Eightfold Path. It means to achieve Perfect Vision by one means or another, and then transform our whole being in accordance with that vision.

The Nature of Existence

What then is Perfect Vision? In the literature of Buddhism there are many expositions of Right Understanding, as Perfect Vision is generally called. One might even say there are too many, for some expositions are not very helpful, and may even be misleading. Under the heading of Right Understanding some writers on Buddhism would apparently like to include the whole of Buddhist doctrine. Whatever could not be included under any other heading is squeezed in here. 'After all', they seem to think, 'it is all a matter of Right Understanding: it is all something to be *understood*.' So in it all goes—the whole doctrine, the whole teaching, the whole philosophy. This tends to create the wrong impression. I have found that students of Buddhism often think that Right Understanding, as the first step of the Noble Eightfold Path, means making a thorough study of the whole of Buddhist thought, and taking a sort of Ph.D. in Buddhist philosophy. They think that before you can start walking on the Noble Eightfold Path you have to learn all about the Mādhyamikas and the Yogācārins, the Sarvāstivādins and the Sautrāntikas, as well as about the T'ien T'ai school and the Avataṁsaka school, and so on. Only then, they think, can you put your foot on the Path and start practising Buddhism.

But really it is not like that at all. *Samyag-dṛṣṭi*, it must be emphasized, is just Perfect Vision. It has nothing to do with the study of the schools of Buddhist philosophy. It is a *vision*, and as such something direct and immediate, and more of the nature of a spiritual experience than an intellectual understanding. Of course the experience, the insight, can be *expressed* intellectually, in terms of doctrinal concepts, philosophical systems, and so on, but it is not identical with these. The vision itself stands apart, stands above.

So what is this Perfect Vision? One may say it is a vision of the nature of existence, but what does this vision reveal? What *is* the nature of existence? This question is difficult to answer because it is easy—only too easy—to answer. I am not being paradoxical. What I mean is that only too many concepts lie ready to hand. There is so much Buddhist philosophy available. We can so easily use a few technical terms, refer to this system or that, and say *this* is the nature of existence according to Buddhism. But this is too slick, too easy. We must beware of the temptation to produce our concepts too readily. What we are trying to communicate is not simply a set of ideas, not a system of philosophy in the academic sense, but what the Buddha himself, in his own language, quite unambiguously called *dṛṣṭi*—a *vision*.

There are two principal ways a vision can be communicated—through images and through concepts. In Buddhism there are three main images of the nature of existence. These are the Wheel of Life, the Buddha, and the Path. Since these images communicate a *vision*, it is helpful, in absorbing that communication, if we can 'get the picture', instead of just 'thinking' them in an abstract manner and assuming they have been understood.

The Wheel of Life

The Wheel of Life comprises four concentric circles. Within the central circle, which forms the hub of the wheel, are three animals, a cock, a snake, and a pig, each biting the tail of the animal in front. These animals represent the three poisons of greed, hatred, and delusion which control our minds and make the whole wheel of mundane existence revolve. Outside the hub is a second circle, divided into two equal segments, one black and one white. The white half represents the good or ethical path leading upwards, to states of happiness. The black half represents the bad or unethical path leading downwards, to states of misery. The third circle is divided into six segments representing the different 'worlds' or spheres of existence within which, according to Buddhism, sentient beings are continuously reborn. These six worlds are those of the gods, titans, hungry ghosts, hell beings, animals, and humans. The outermost circle of the wheel, which forms the rim, is divided into twelve segments. These are the twelve *nidānas*, or links in the process which is called Dependent Origination, or Conditioned Co-production (*pratītya-samutpāda*). These show in detail the whole process of birth, life, death, and rebirth.

This is the first great image, the first great symbol. This is what we begin to see when we have a vision of the nature of existence. We see the whole of mundane conditioned existence going round like a great wheel—a Wheel of Life, a Wheel of Death—with ourselves as well as all other sentient beings caught up in it. We see that the Wheel of Life in fact *is* us, *is* sentient, conditioned existence.

The Buddha

The Buddha is usually depicted seated on a lotus flower or beneath the Bodhi tree, the 'Tree of Enlightenment', with its great spreading branches and its canopy of beautiful heart-shaped leaves, his body radiating light of various colours. There are also more elaborate versions of this image. One of the best known is the mandala of the Five Buddhas, which comes from the more esoteric teaching. In the centre of this mandala is the White Buddha, with the Dark Blue Buddha to the east, the Yellow Buddha to the south, the Red Buddha to the west, and the Green Buddha to the north. There are even more elaborate versions of the image in the form of 'The Pure Land', or 'The Happy Land'—*Sukhāvatī*—with its presiding Buddha flanked by his attendant Bodhisattvas, its rows of wonderful jewel-trees, its magical singing birds, and many other marvels.

The Path

The path of spiritual progress—or spiral path—connects the two images we have already described, that is to say it leads up from the Wheel of Life to the Buddha, or to the mandala of the Five Buddhas.

These then are the three great images through which Buddhism communicates its vision of existence. Perfect Vision is a vision, first of all, of our actual present state of bondage to conditioned existence as represented by the Wheel of Life. It is also a vision of our potential future state of Enlightenment as represented by the Buddha, or the mandala of Buddhas, or the Pure Land. Finally it is a vision of the path or way leading from the one to the other—a vision, if you like, of the whole future course of evolution.

The Buddhist vision of the nature of existence can also be communicated in terms of concepts—though perhaps less vividly than through images. Perfect Vision is thus traditionally explained in terms of seeing and understanding the truth of certain doctrinal categories, and for completeness I shall deal briefly with four of the most important of these: the Four Noble Truths, the Three Characteristics of Conditioned Existence, karma and rebirth, and the Four *Śūnyatās*. In grappling with these conceptual explanations we should remember that here we are not concerned with any merely theoretical understanding. We are trying, with the help of these doctrinal categories, to obtain a glimpse of the Truth—to achieve some kind of vision of the nature of existence.

The Four Noble Truths
Perfect Vision is usually explained in the doctrinal manuals as a vision or an understanding of the Four Noble Truths. These are:
1. The Truth of suffering, unsatisfactoriness, or disharmony, which we see all around us and also experience within ourselves;
2. The Truth of the cause of suffering, which is selfish craving or 'thirst', both within ourselves and within others;
3. The Truth of the cessation of suffering, the total eradication of suffering which is synonymous with the state of Enlightenment or Buddhahood; and
4. The Truth of the way leading to the cessation of suffering, which is the Noble Eightfold Path.
    It is interesting to note that the first and second Noble Truths, that is to say suffering and the cause of suffering,

together correspond to the image of the Wheel of Life. Suffering being the effect, and craving the cause, there is here a cause–effect, action–reaction type of relationship. In other words there is the same cyclical pattern as represented by the Wheel of Life. The third Noble Truth, the cessation of suffering, corresponds to the image of the Buddha, or the mandala of the Five Buddhas. The fourth Noble Truth—the Eightfold Path—corresponds to the image of the spiral path. We therefore see that the Four Noble Truths present conceptually what our three images present in visual terms. Both express the same vision: a vision of the nature of conditioned existence, of the Unconditioned, and of the Path leading from the one to the other.

The Three Characteristics of Conditioned Existence

The Three Characteristics of Conditioned Existence are that it is suffering, that it is impermanent, and that it is devoid of true selfhood.

1. Conditioned Existence is Suffering

According to Buddhism there are three kinds of suffering. Firstly there is actual suffering, as when you have a toothache or cut your finger. Secondly there is potential suffering, as when you possess something which is a source of enjoyment to you: even though it is a source of enjoyment at present, potentially it is suffering, in that you may—indeed must—have to give it up one day. Finally there is metaphysical suffering, which arises because nothing mundane, earthly, or conditioned can give full or final satisfaction to the human heart and spirit—because true and lasting satisfaction can be found only in the Unconditioned, in Truth itself. Everything short of that is therefore in a sense a subtle form of suffering. This means that one will never be truly happy until one is Enlightened.

2. *Conditioned Existence is Impermanent*

As we know only too well, every conditioned thing is impermanent. Every day, every hour, every minute we are being made aware of the fact that nothing lasts, nothing stays. Everything flows on. Nothing remains the same even for two consecutive seconds. We are growing old all the time, and the things around us are wearing out all the time. There is no stability, no security. We like to think we have got something for ever, but this 'for ever' may be a few years, or a few days, or a few hours—even a few minutes. This is one very important aspect of Perfect Vision as applied to mundane things: seeing, clearly and steadily, that everything is impermanent, everything transient, and that you cannot hold on to anything for very long.

3. *Conditioned Existence is Devoid of True Selfhood*

This is a rather difficult and abstruse aspect of Perfect Vision that needs at least a whole chapter to itself. All that can be said here is that nowhere in conditioned existence, or in ourselves as conditioned phenomena, do we find true being, true individuality, or reality of any sort. If we look at ourselves we become aware, very often, of how empty, unreal, and hollow we are—that our thoughts are not real thoughts, our emotions are not real emotions. We do not feel real, genuine, or authentic within ourselves. In fact we shall not find genuineness, or authenticity, or true selfhood on the level of the mundane or the conditioned at all, but only on the level of Unconditioned Reality.

Karma and Rebirth

This doctrinal category, or expression of Perfect Vision in conceptual terms, is presented very vividly, sometimes almost pictorially, in the Buddhist Scriptures. There it is said of the Buddha and other Enlightened beings that on the eve of their Enlightenment they saw passing before their eyes a great panorama of births, deaths, and rebirths, not only of themselves but of other living beings—in fact, of all living beings. Tracing the whole process of karma from one life to another they saw very clearly how people either suffer or find happiness as a consequence of their previous actions, and how they are reborn in accordance with the way in which they lived their past lives.

The doctrinal categories so far mentioned—the Four Noble Truths, the Three Characteristics of Conditioned Existence, and karma and rebirth—are all attempts to give conceptual expression to a Perfect Vision of the nature of existence. They are all doctrinal categories derived from the Hīnayāna tradition. But Perfect Vision can also be expressed, more profoundly perhaps, in terms of the doctrinal categories of the Mahāyāna. One of the most important of these is the Four Śūnyatās.

The Four Śūnyatās
Śūnyatā literally means voidness or emptiness, but it signifies much more than either of these words conveys. According to context Śūnyatā can mean 'real', or 'unreal', or 'neither real nor unreal'—so it is quite a bewildering word! Let us then go through the four kinds of *sunyata*, bearing in mind that they are not just figments of the metaphysical imagination, but attempts to communicate in conceptual terms a *vision*, or something the Enlightened Ones have actually seen and experienced.

1. Saṁskṛta Śūnyatā—The Emptiness of the Conditioned
The Emptiness of the Conditioned means that conditioned, phenomenal, relative existence is devoid of the characteristics of the Unconditioned, the Absolute, the Truth. The characteristics of the Unconditioned are first of all happiness, secondly permanence (not that it persists in time, but that it occupies, as it were, a dimension within

which time itself does not exist), and thirdly true being, Ultimate Reality.

Conditioned existence is devoid of these characteristics of the Unconditioned. It is, on the contrary, unsatisfactory, impermanent, and not wholly real. For this reason the conditioned is said to be empty of the Unconditioned, Samsara empty of Nirvana. What this means in practical terms is that we should not expect to find in the flux of relative existence what only the Unconditioned, the Absolute, can give us.

2. Asaṁskṛta Śūnyatā—*The Emptiness of the Unconditioned*
The Emptiness of the Unconditioned means that the Unconditioned is devoid of the characteristics of the conditioned. In the Unconditioned, in Nirvana, there is no unhappiness or suffering, no impermanence, and no unreality, which are characteristics of the conditioned, but only the opposite characteristics in their fullness. Just as in the conditioned one will not find the Unconditioned, so in the Unconditioned one will not find the conditioned.

These first two kinds of *Śūnyatā* are common to all forms of Buddhism. Being mutually exclusive they obviously represent a comparatively dualistic approach, but this is necessary as the working basis of our spiritual life in its early stages. We have to make this distinction, to think 'Here is the conditioned and there the Unconditioned; I want to get from here to there.' We cannot help thinking in these terms.

According to the Hinayāna tradition, Wisdom—seeing things as they are in reality—consists in seeing objects and persons in the external world, as well as all mental phenomena, in terms of what are technically known as *dharmas*. *Dharma* has many meanings. It usually means 'teaching' or 'doctrine', but here it means something quite different. According to the Hinayāna there is in reality no such objective existent or thing as, for instance, a house, a tree, or a man. If we look at these things closely, if we examine and analyse them, they become, as it were, insubstantial. Ultimately they tend to reduce themselves to a flux, a flow of irreducible elements which are impersonal, non-substantial, psycho-physical processes. These are known as *dharmas*.

According to the Mahāyāna however, Wisdom consists in reducing the *dharmas* themselves to *Śūnyatā*. When we see things in terms of objects and persons, this, the Mahā yāna would say, is on account of our gross delusion. And this gross delusion is removed by our learning to see these objects and persons in terms of *dharmas*. But the Mahāyāna goes on to say that even seeing things in terms of *dharmas* is not to see them in their ultimate reality. We see things in terms of *dharmas* on account of subtle delusion, and this too must be removed. We remove it by knowing, by seeing, that the *dharmas* themselves are *Śūnyatā*. Wisdom in the Mahāyāna sense is known as the Perfection of Wisdom, the *Prajñā Pāramitā*. The Perfection of Wisdom is concerned with seeing *Śūnyatā* everywhere, at all times, under all circumstances.

The third and fourth kinds of *Śūnyatā* are peculiar to the Mahāyāna.

3. Mahā Śūnyatā—*The Great Emptiness*

In the Mahāyāna, 'mahā', in addition to its more literal meaning of 'great', always means 'pertaining to *Śūnyatā*'. The Mahāyāna is 'The Vehicle of *Śūnyatā*'.

In the *Mahā Śūnyatā* or Great Emptiness we see that the distinction between the conditioned and the Unconditioned is not ultimately valid—that it is a product of dualistic thinking. We may spend ten, fifteen, twenty years of our spiritual life working on the assumption that the conditioned is the conditioned and the Unconditioned the Unconditioned. But eventually we have to learn to see the 'emptiness' of the distinction between the two—to see that this distinction is to be transcended. We have to see—to *experience*, not just speculate about, or understand intellectually or theoretically—that *rūpa* and *Śūnyatā*, form and voidness, the conditioned and the Unconditioned, ordinary beings and Buddhas, are of one and the same essence, one and the same ultimate Reality. This is *Mahā Śūnyatā*, the Great Emptiness in which all distinctions and all dualities are obliterated. It is this great void into which people, even spiritual people, are so afraid of disappearing. They want to cling to their dualistic ways of thinking —self and others, this and that—but eventually these must all be swallowed up. This is the Tiger's Cave which is remarkable for the fact that many tracks lead to it, but none come out. That is why one wants to go into it!

4. Śūnyatā Śūnyatā—*The Emptiness of Emptiness*
The Emptiness of Emptiness tells us that emptiness itself is only a concept, only a word, only a sound. In Maha *Śūnyatā* one is still hanging on to subtle thoughts, subtle dualistic experiences. Even this has to be ultimately abandoned. Then one comes to *Śūnyatā Śūnyatā*, and there is just nothing to be said. All that is left is silence—but a significant silence, a 'thunderous silence'.

All these doctrinal categories, whether of the Hinayāna or of the Mahāyāna, try to give conceptual expression to a vision of the nature of existence. But important as they are we must not dwell upon them too much, or there is a danger that we might confuse Perfect Vision with right understanding in the purely theoretical sense. If I have done nothing else I hope I have at least been able to stress the fact that *samyag-dṛṣṭi* is a vision, an insight, a spiritual experience of the nature of existence, in accordance with which we have to transform our lives, our being, in every aspect, on every level.

In order to avoid concluding this discussion of Perfect Vision with any sort of conceptual emphasis, let me finish with a simile. Imagine we want to make a journey to climb some lofty mountain peak. What do we do? First we study a map of the terrain, of the surrounding foothills, and of the mountain itself. This study of the map corresponds to the theoretical study of Buddhist doctrine, to knowing all about the Mādhyamikas, the Yogācārins, the Sarvāstivādins, and so on. But we have to actually start our journey, we have to get going—we have at least to get to base camp. *This* corresponds to our preliminary practice of the Buddha's teaching. Eventually, after several days, weeks, or months of travelling, we catch a glimpse of the distant mountain peak which is the object of our journey. We have come only a little way, and are still far from the foot of the mountain, but there in the distance we see the shining snow peak. We have a direct perception—a vision—of it, although from a very great distance.

This glimpse of the peak corresponds to Perfect Vision, and it gives us inspiration and encouragement to continue our journey. We can go on from there, keeping our eyes on the peak, never losing sight of it, at least not for more than a few minutes at a time. We may not care how long the journey, how many nights we spend on the way, how difficult the terrain, how hot or cold it is. We may not even care if we are starving, so long as we have our eyes firmly fixed on the peak. We are happy in the knowledge that we are getting nearer day by day, and that one day we shall find ourselves at the foot of the peak. This process of travelling with the peak in view corresponds to traversing the remaining stages of the Noble Eightfold Path. Eventually we may find ourselves on the lower slopes of the mountain. We may even find ourselves on the virgin snows of the peak itself—may find that we have attained Enlightenment, or Buddhahood.

II *Reason and Emotion in the Spiritual Life*
Perfect Emotion

With the second stage of the Noble Eightfold Path we come to one of the most important questions, not to say problems, in the whole of the spiritual life. This is the question of reason and emotion. We all know from our own experience that it is comparatively easy to understand a religious or philosophical teaching intellectually or theoretically. Abstruse, complex, and even intrinsically difficult as it may be, with a little mental exertion and systematic study we can usually manage to understand it without too much trouble. But when it comes to putting that teaching into practice, we find this is a much more difficult matter.

There is an oft-repeated anecdote from Buddhist history which well illustrates this point. It appears that in ancient times Indian monks used to go from India to China in large numbers to preach the Doctrine, and that at one period of Chinese history there was a very pious Chinese emperor who was always eager to welcome great sages and teachers from India. Now one day it so happened that one of the greatest of the Indian teachers turned up in the Chinese capital, and the emperor, as soon as he heard the news, was very pleased indeed. He thought he would have a wonderful philosophical discussion with this newlyarrived teacher. So the teacher was invited to the palace, where he was received with due pomp and ceremony. When all the formalities were over and the teacher and the emperor had taken their seats, the emperor put his first question. 'Tell me,' he said, 'what is the fundamental principle of Buddhism?' and sat back, waiting to get the answer straight from the horse's mouth, as it were. The teacher replied, 'Ceasing to do evil; learning to be good; purifying the heart—this is the fundamental principle of Buddhism.' The emperor was rather taken aback. He had heard all that before. (We have usually heard it all before!) So he said, 'Is that all? Is *that* the fundamental principle of Buddhism?' 'Yes,' replied the sage, 'That's all. Cease to do evil; learn to be good; purify the heart. That is indeed the fundamental principle of Buddhism.' 'But this is so simple that even a child of three can understand it,' protested the emperor. 'Yes, your majesty,' said the teacher, 'that is quite true. It is so simple that even a child of three can understand it, but so difficult that even an old man of eighty cannot put it into practice.'

This story illustrates the great difference that exists between understanding and practice. We find it easy simply to *understand*. We can understand the Abhidharma; we can understand the Mādhyamika; we can understand the Yogācāra; we can understand Plato; we can understand Aristotle; we can understand the Four Gospels; we can understand everything. But to put into practice even a little of all this knowledge and make it operative in our lives, this we find very difficult indeed. In the famous words of St Paul, 'The good that I would I do not: but the evil which I would not, that I do.'* He knows what he ought to do but is unable to do it; and that which he knows he should not do, that he cannot help doing. Again we see this tremendous, this terrible disparity between understanding and practice.

This state of affairs is not exceptional. It is not just a

Romans VII, 19

question of the Chinese emperor or St Paul. All religious people find themselves at some time or other, sometimes for years together, in this quite terrible and tragic predicament. They know the truth rationally, they know it from A to Z and from Z back to A. They can talk about it, write about it, give lectures about it. But they are unable to put it into practice. For those who are sincere this can be a source of great suffering. They may feel, 'I know this very well, and see it so clearly; but I am unable to put it into practice, unable to carry it out.' It is as though there were some blind spot in themselves, some 'X-factor' which was obstructing their efforts all the time. No sooner do they lift themselves up a few inches than they slip back what sometimes feels like a mile.

Why does this happen? Why is there this terrible gulf, this terrible chasm, between our theory and our practice, our understanding and our operation? Why are most of us most of the time unable to act in accordance with what we *know* is true, what we *know* is right? Why do we fail so miserably again and yet again?

The answer to this question is to be sought in the very depths of human nature. We may say that we 'know' something, but we know it only with the conscious mind, with the rational part of ourselves. We know it theoretically, intellectually, abstractly. But we must recollect that man is not just his conscious mind. He is not all reason— though he may like to think he is. There is a another part of us, a much larger part than we care to admit, which is no less important than our reason. This part is made up of instinct, of emotion, of volition, and is more unconscious than conscious. And this wider, deeper, and no less important part of ourselves is not touched at all by our rational or intellectual knowledge, but goes its own way, as it were dragging the mental part, still protesting, along with it.

Thus we see that we cannot go against the emotions. The emotions are stronger than reason. If we want to put into practice what we know to be right, what we know to be true, we have to enlist, in one way or another, the co-operation of the emotions. We have to be able to tap those deeper sources within ourselves and harness them, also, to our spiritual life, so that we may *implement* what we know to be right and true. *For most of us the central problem of the spiritual life is to find emotional equivalents for our intellectual understanding.* Until we have done this no further spiritual progress is possible. This is why Perfect Emotion comes as the second stage, or second aspect, of the Noble Eightfold Path, immediately after Perfect Vision.

Samyak-samkalpa—Perfect Emotion

In Sanskrit the second limb of the Noble Eightfold Path is called *Samyak-samkalpa* (Pali *sammā-saṅkappa*). *Samyak-samkalpa* could provisionally be translated as Right Resolve, but this is far from adequate. As we have seen in connection with the first stage of the Noble Eightfold Path, *samyak* means whole, perfect, integral, complete. Translators usually render *samkalpa* as thought, intention, purpose, or plan, but none of these is very satisfactory.

Samkalpa, a word which exists in the same form in modern Indian languages, really means 'will'. *Samyak-samkalpa* is not just Right Resolve. It is more like Perfect Will or Integral Emotion, and it represents the harmonization of the whole emotional and volitional side of our being with Perfect Vision, our vision of the true nature of existence.

We have already seen that the Noble Eightfold Path consists of two sections, the Path of Vision and the Path of Transformation. The Path of Vision corresponds to the first stage of the Eightfold Path, Perfect Vision, while the Path of Transformation corresponds to all the other stages.

Thus Perfect Emotion is the first stage of the Path of Transformation, and represents the transformation of our emotional nature in accordance with Perfect Vision. In a sense, Perfect Emotion mediates between Perfect Vision and the last six stages of the Path, because we cannot follow that Path—cannot really practise Right Speech, Right Action, and so on—until we have transformed our whole emotional nature, and in that way derived energy for the remaining stages of the Path. This is why the problem of reason and emotion is central in the spiritual life. Putting it simply, there is really no spiritual life until the heart is also involved. No matter how active the brain is, or how much we have understood intellectually, until the heart is involved and we begin to *feel* what we have understood—until our *emotions* are engaged—there is no spiritual life, properly speaking.

Now what is Perfect Emotion? Before entering into this question I want to clear up two possible misunderstandings.

Firstly, I have spoken of involving the emotions in the spiritual life, but this is not to be understood in a negative sense. It does not mean the involvement of crude, untransformed emotions with irrational, pseudo-religious concepts and attitudes. For example, suppose somebody hears that church halls are being used for dances on Sunday evenings. He gets very hot under the collar, gets very upset that the Sabbath is being desecrated, that the church hall is being used for such immoral purposes. In his indignation and excitement he writes a letter to the *Times* denouncing the immorality of the younger generation and predicting the downfall of civilization as we know it. Now you may think that he is really worked up, and that his emotions are involved in a religious issue of sorts. But this is not Perfect Emotion, because such feelings are not expressions of Perfect Vision. They are based only on a bundle of prejudices and rationalizations held in the name of religion. We see other examples of this kind of feeling and behaviour in those famous institutions the Inquisition and the Crusades. A great deal of emotion was involved in these, and some people think of it as religious emotion, but again it was not Perfect Emotion in the Buddhist sense. Although ostensibly connected with religion, there was no element of Perfect Vision present. This is the first kind of misunderstanding to be guarded against.

Secondly, it is not possible to transform one's emotional nature by strength of intellectual or rational conviction. We cannot reason or argue ourselves into a state of Perfect Emotion. Our emotions can be thoroughly transformed only by Perfect Vision, which is a spiritual insight or spiritual experience.

Perfect Emotion represents the descent of Perfect Vision into our emotional nature in such a way as to transform it totally. It has a positive aspect and a negative aspect.

The negative aspect of Perfect Emotion
The negative side of Perfect Emotion consists of what we call in Sanskrit *naiṣkramya* (Pali *nekkhamma*), *avyāpāda* (Pali and Skt), and *avihiṁsa* (Pali and Skt): 'non-desire', 'non-hate', and 'non-cruelty'.

Naiṣkramya, or 'non-desire'.
Naiṣkramya means non-desire, renunciation, giving up, or giving away. This is an extremely important element of Perfect Emotion. As we have seen, Perfect Emotion follows Perfect Vision—vision into the true nature of things, or into the nature of existence. One aspect of Perfect Vision is Insight into the unsatisfactory nature of conditioned existence, or life as we usually live it. This sort of Insight should by its very nature have some kind of practical result. *Naiṣkramya* or non-desire *is* that practical result. It

represents a decrease of craving as a result of our vision of the true nature of conditioned things. We see their inadequacy, and so we become less attached to them, and crave for them less. Our tight grip on worldly things, usually so convulsive, starts to relax.

Since craving is the basic unwholesome mental state, we should examine ourselves in this respect, and ask ourselves the very pertinent question: 'Since I started taking Buddhism seriously, what have I given up?' If we have developed a degree of insight, if we are convinced not just intellectually but spiritually that the things of this world are not fully satisfactory, then our hold on them should have loosened. Buddhism should make a difference to our lives. We should not be going along in the same old way as before. If our lives have not changed it means there has not been even a glimpse of Perfect Vision, and that our interest so far, although it may be a genuine one, is no more than intellectual, theoretical, or even academic.

There is no single uniform pattern of renunciation. No one has the right to say that because another has not given up this or that particular thing they therefore have no Perfect Vision and are not practising Buddhists. Different people will give up different things first, but the net result must be the same: to make life simpler and less cluttered. Most of us have so many things we do not really need. If here and now you were to take a piece of paper and write down all the unnecessary things you possess it would probably be a very long list. But you would probably think a long time before actually giving any of them away.

Sometimes people think in terms of sacrifice: that with a great painful wrench you give something up; but it should not be like that. In Buddhism there is really no such thing as 'giving up' in this way. From the Buddhist point of view what is required is not so much *giving* up as *growing* up. It is no sacrifice to the adolescent to give up the child's toys. And in the same way it should not be a sacrifice for the spiritually mature person, or for a person who is at least verging on spiritual maturity, to give up the toys with which people usually amuse themselves. I do not suggest that we do this in a dramatic or violent fashion; not like the gentleman I heard about on the radio the other day, who climbed up the Eiffel Tower and threw his television set from the viewing platform. (He was protesting against the quality of French television programmes, but at least his action indicated a certain degree of detachment from his television set!) The point to be made is that if we really have some degree of vision of the true nature of existence, and have really to some extent seen the inadequacy of material, worldly things, then our hold on them will be relaxed, and we will be quite willing and happy to let at least some of them go—to have just *one* car perhaps!

Avyāpāda *or 'non-hate'.*
Avyāpāda is the negative form of *vyāpāda*, which literally means 'doing harm', therefore 'hatred'. Hatred, as we know, is closely connected with craving. Very often we find that hatred or antagonism, in any of its numerous forms, is at bottom frustrated craving. We see this very clearly in the case of children. If you do not give a child something that he wants very much, he flies into a rage or tantrum. Adults do not usually do this. *Their* reactions are not usually so simple and uncomplicated, for their cravings are in any case much more complex. They do not crave simply for material things, but instead for success, recognition, praise, and affection. When these things are denied, especially when denied a long time, then a mood of frustration sets in. This produces in many people a deep bitterness, indulgence in constant criticism of others, fault-finding, nagging, and all sorts of other negative activities. But with the decrease of craving, and the loosening of our

grip on at least some material things, hatred also decreases, because the possibility of frustration is progressively reduced. So another question we should ask ourselves is: 'Since I started taking a real interest in Buddhism, have I become at least a little better tempered?' If even within a Buddhist circle there are little tiffs and misunderstandings it means that some people, at least, are not putting their Buddhism into practice: that they have no Perfect Vision, and no Perfect Emotion.

Avihiṁsa *or non-cruelty.*
Hiṁsa is violence or harm, and *vihiṁsa*—of which *avihiṁsa* is the negative form—is deliberate infliction of pain and suffering. *Vihiṁsa* is a very strong word in Pali and Sanskrit, and is best translated as 'cruelty'. Its connection with hatred is obvious, but it is much worse than simple hatred because it generally connotes a wanton infliction of pain, or a positive pleasure in the infliction of pain. In the Mahāyāna form of Buddhism cruelty in this sense is considered the greatest of all possible sins. Often, of course, especially in the case of children, cruelty is due to simple thoughtlessness. Children may not realize that other forms of life suffer. Therefore it is important for those who have dealings with the young, whether as parents or educators, to try to instil into children a sense of the fact that living beings are *living* beings like themselves, and suffer if you poke your finger in their eye or stick a pin into a sensitive place. Children may not realize this, and if they see an animal that they have just kicked wriggling and howling they may simply be amused, not understanding that pain has been inflicted.

An incident from the life of the Buddha illustrates this point. Once when the Buddha was going on his alms-round he found a gang of boys tormenting a crow which had broken its wing, in the way that boys are prone to do,

41

and enjoying the 'fun'. He stopped and asked them, 'If you are struck, do you feel hurt?' and they said 'Yes.' The Buddha then said, 'Well, when you hit the crow, the bird also feels hurt. When you yourself know how unpleasant it is to experience pain, why do you inflict it on another living being?' A simple lesson, that a child can understand and act upon, but a lesson that needs to be learnt at an early age, for if this sort of behaviour is not checked early in life it can get worse and worse and culminate in quite horrible atrocities.

Hogarth's engravings of the Four Stages of Cruelty vividly portray this frightening reality: the first shows young Tom Nero and his friends tormenting a dog; in the second, now grown up, Tom is flogging a horse to death; in the third he is caught in the act of murder, while in the fourth his corpse is being dissected by a band of surgeons after he has been hanged. We should not make light of the connection between these stages. When we see a child tormenting an animal we should not think that it does not matter, that the child will grow out of it. We should be careful to explain to him what he is actually doing, for it is in this way that the seeds of violence and cruelty are sown. So here is another question for us to ask ourselves: 'Since I took up Buddhism, have I become less cruel?' And cruelty, let us remember, is not just physical. It can also be verbal. Many people indulge in harsh, unkind, cutting, sarcastic speech, and this too is a form of cruelty. It is a form of cruelty in which a Buddhist, or one in whom Perfect Vision and Perfect Emotion have arisen, should find it impossible to indulge.

In the same way, it should be impossible for a Buddhist to indulge in blood sports. You may tell me you know the Abhidharma very well, but if at the same time you are engaging in blood sports every Sunday morning I shall not take your knowledge of the Abhidharma very seriously.

This is an extreme case. Most people do not indulge in blood sports nowadays, though some unfortunately still do, and even try to defend the practice. But from a Buddhist point of view—from the point of view of Perfect Vision and Perfect Emotion—blood sports are quite inadmissible, because of the very definite and wanton cruelty involved.

The question of cruelty brings us to the issue of vegetarianism. Many people feel that they cannot eat meat or fish because this would make them accomplices in often deliberate and wanton acts of cruelty. Although there is no hard or fast rule that if you want to be a Buddhist you *must* be a vegetarian, yet a sincere Buddhist—one who is trying to follow the Eightfold Path, and in whom Perfect Vision has arisen and Perfect Emotion is beginning to stir—will certainly make some move in this direction. The reason for this is that as one progresses on the spiritual path one's feelings become more and more sensitive, so that eventually things like eating meat just drop away of their own accord.

The positive aspect of Perfect Emotion
The positive side of Perfect Emotion consists of a number of wholesome emotions, all connected. These include the positive counterparts of renunciation, non-hatred, and non-cruelty, known in Sanskrit and Pali as *dāna*, *maitrī* (Pali *mettā*), and *karuṇā*, that is to say, giving, love, and compassion. Also included are *muditā* or sympathetic joy, *upekṣā* (Pali *upekkhā*) or tranquillity, and *śraddhā* (Pali *saddhā*), or faith and devotion. *Maitrī, karuṇā, muditā,* and *upekṣā* collectively form the *brahma vihāras* or 'sublime states'.

Dāna, *or giving.*
In a sense *dāna* or giving is the basic Buddhist virtue, without which you can hardly call yourself a Buddhist.

Dāna consists not so much in the act of giving as in the feeling of wanting to give, of wanting to share what you have with other people. This feeling of wanting to give or share is often the first manifestation of the spiritual life—the first sign that craving and detachment have decreased to some extent. *Dāna* is discussed at great length in Buddhist literature, and many different forms are enumerated.

First, there is *the giving of material things*, or sharing what you have of the good things of life: food, clothing, and so on. Some people in the East make it a practice to try to give something of a material nature every day, be it food to a beggar, a small sum of money, or just a cup of tea, so that every day something is given, or something shared, on the material plane.

Secondly there is *the giving of time, energy, and thought*. Time is a very precious thing, and if we give some of it to help other people this is also a form of *dāna*, giving, or generosity.

There is also *the giving of knowledge*, in the sense of the giving of culture and education. This has always ranked very highly in Buddhist countries. Intellectual acquisitions should not be kept to oneself, but should be shared with all. All should be able to benefit from them. This was particularly emphasized in Buddhist India, because the Brahmin caste, the priestly caste of Hinduism, invariably sought to monopolize knowledge and keep other castes in a state of ignorance and subservience. Buddhism has always stressed that knowledge, even secular knowledge and secular culture, should not be a monopoly of any particular caste or class of people, but should be disseminated amongst the whole community.

Another important kind of giving mentioned in Buddhist literature is *the giving of fearlessness*. This might seem a rather strange kind of 'gift'. You cannot hand anyone fearlessness on a plate, or wrapped up in a little parcel tied with ribbon. But you can share your own confidence with other people. You can create among people a feeling of fearlessness or security by your very presence, your very attitude. Buddhism attaches great importance to this ability to reassure people by your mere presence. According to Buddhism this form of *dāna* is an important contribution to the life of the community.

Yet another form of *dāna* which is mentioned in Buddhist literature is *the giving of life and limb*. For the sake of other people, or for the sake of the Dharma, the Teaching, one should be prepared to sacrifice one's own limbs, even one's own life. *Dāna*, giving or generosity, can go as far as this.

Finally, surpassing even the giving of one's own life, there is what is called in Buddhism *the giving of the gift of the Dharma*: the gift of truth itself; the gift of the knowledge, or understanding, of the way to Enlightenment, Emancipation, Buddhahood, or Nirvana. The gift of this sort of knowledge surpasses all other gifts whatever.

These are just some of the things which one can give, and looking at them we begin to see how vast and comprehensive the practice of giving can be. According to Buddhist teaching we should be giving in some way or other, on some level or other, all the time. In the Buddhist East *dāna* or giving penetrates and permeates all aspects of social and religious life. If you are going to a temple, for instance, you don't go empty handed: you take flowers, candles, and incense, and offer them there. In the same way if you go to see a friend, even if the visit is only a casual one, you always take a present. When I was staying in Kalimpong, and mixing a great deal with Tibetans, I found that this was absolutely *de rigueur*. A friend would not think of appearing on your doorstep without a tin of biscuits or some other gift under his arm. In this way the spirit of giving permeates all aspects of life in many

Buddhist countries. No doubt all this does sometimes become just a custom, and often there might not be much feeling attached to it. But nonetheless when you are giving all the time in one form or another it does have some influence upon the mind—even if you are doing it only because you are expected to. You get into the habit of giving and sharing, and of thinking a little bit about others, instead of all the time about yourself.

Maitrī, *or love*

The Sanskrit word *maitrī* is derived from *mitra*, which means friend. According to the Buddhist texts *maitrī* is that love which one feels for a very near and dear, very intimate, friend, but extended to include all beings. The English words 'friend' and 'friendship' nowadays have a rather tepid connotation, and friendship is regarded as a somewhat feeble emotion. But it is not like that in the East. There *maitrī* or friendship is seen as a very powerful and positive emotion, usually defined as an overwhelming desire for the happiness and well-being of the other person, not just in the material sense, but in the spiritual sense as well. Buddhist literature and teaching exhort us over and over again to develop this feeling we have for our very closest friends to include all living beings. This attitude is summed up in the phrase '*Sabbe sattā sukhī hontu*' or 'May all beings be happy!' which ideally represents the heartfelt wish of all Buddhists. If we have this heartfelt feeling—not just the idea of the feeling but the feeling itself—then we have *maitrī*.

In Buddhism the development of *maitrī* is not just left to chance. Some people think that either you have got love for others or you haven't, and that if you haven't that's too bad, because there's nothing you can do about it. But Buddhism does not look at it like that. In Buddhism there are definite exercises, definite practices, for the development of *maitrī* or love—what we call *maitrī-bhāvanā* (Pali *mettā bhāvanā*). These are not easy. We do not find it easy to develop love, but if we persist and succeed the experience is very rewarding.

Karuṇā, *or compassion*

Compassion is of course closely connected with love. Love changes into compassion when confronted by the suffering of a loved person. If you love someone and see them suffering your love is at once transformed into an overwhelming feeling of compassion. According to Buddhism *Karuṇā* or compassion is the most spiritual of all the emotions, and it is the emotion that particularly characterizes all the Buddhas and Bodhisattvas. Certain Bodhisattvas, however, especially embody compassion: for instance Avalokiteśvara, 'the Lord Who Looks Down (in Compassion)', who among the Bodhisattvas is the principal 'incarnation' or archetype of compassion. There are many different forms of Avalokiteśvara. One of the most interesting is the eleven-headed and thousand-armed form which, though it may look rather bizarre to us, from a symbolic point of view is very expressive. The eleven heads represent the fact that Compassion looks in all eleven directions of space—that is, in all possible directions—while the thousand arms represent his ceaseless compassionate activity.

There is an interesting story about how this particular form arose—a story that is not just 'mythology', but based upon the facts of spiritual psychology. Once upon a time, it is said, Avalokiteśvara was contemplating the sorrows of sentient beings. As he looked out over the world, he saw people suffering in so many ways: some dying untimely deaths by fire, shipwreck, and execution; others suffering the pangs of bereavement, loss, illness, hunger, thirst, and starvation. A tremendous compassion welled up in his heart, becoming so unbearably intense that his head shivered into pieces. It shivered, in fact, into eleven pieces, which became eleven heads looking in the eleven directions of space, and a thousand arms were manifested to help all those beings who were suffering. Thus this very beautiful conception of the eleven-headed and thousand-armed Avalokiteśvara is an attempt to express the essence of compassion, to show how the compassionate heart feels for the sorrows and suffering of the world.

Another very beautiful Bodhisattva figure embodying Compassion, this time in female form, is Tārā, whose name means 'The Saviouress' or 'The Star'. A very beautiful legend relates how she was born from the tears of Avalokiteśvara as he wept over the sorrows and miseries of the world.

We may think of these legends as being just stories, and the sophisticated may even smile at them a little. But they are not just stories—not even illustrative stories. They are of real, deep, symbolic, even archetypal significance, and represent, embodied in concrete form, the nature of Compassion.

In the Mahāyāna form of Buddhism, that is to say in the teaching of the 'Great Way', the highest possible importance is attached to Compassion. In one of the Mahāyāna sutras, in fact, the Buddha is represented as saying that the Bodhisattva—the one who aspires to be a Buddha—should not be taught too many things. If he is taught only Compassion, learns only Compassion, that is quite enough. No need for him to know about conditioned co-production, or about the Mādhyamika, or the Yogācāra, or the Abhidharma—or even the Eightfold Path. If the Bodhisattva knows only compassion, has a heart filled with nothing but compassion, that is enough. In other texts the Buddha says that if one has only compassion for the sufferings of other living beings, then in due course all other virtues, all other spiritual qualities and attainments, even Enlightenment itself, will follow.

This is illustrated by a very moving story from Japan. We are told there was a young man who was a great wastrel. After running through all his money, and having a good time, he became thoroughly disgusted with everything, including himself. In this mood he decided that there was only one thing he could do, and that was to enter the Zen monastery and become a monk. This was his last resort. He didn't really *want* to become a monk, but there was nothing else left for him. So along to the Zen monastery he went. I suppose he knelt outside in the snow for three days, in the way we are told applicants have to kneel. But in the end the abbot agreed to see him. The abbot was a grim old soul. He listened to what the young man had to say, himself not saying very much, but when the young man had told him everything, he said, 'Hmm, well … is there *anything* you are good at?' The young man thought, and finally said, 'Yes, I'm not so bad at chess.' So the abbot called his attendant and told him to fetch a certain monk.

The monk came. He was an old man, and had been a monk for many years. Then the abbot said to the attendant, 'Bring my sword.' So the sword was brought and placed before the abbot. The abbot then said to the young man and the old monk, 'You two will now play a game of chess. Whoever loses, I will cut off his head with this sword!' They looked at him, and they saw that he meant it. So the young man made his first move. The old monk, who was not a bad player, made his. The young man made his next move. The old monk made his. After a little while the young man felt the perspiration pouring down his back and trickling over his heels. So he concentrated: he put everything he had into that game, and managed to beat back the old monk's attack. Then he drew a great breath of relief, 'Ah, the game isn't going too badly!' But just then, when he was sure he would win, he looked up, and he saw the face of that old monk. As I have said, he was an old man, and had been a monk many years—maybe twenty or thirty, or even forty years. He had undergone much suffering, had performed many austerities. He had meditated very much. His face was thin and worn and austere.

The young man suddenly thought, 'I have been an absolute wastrel! My life is no use to anybody. This monk has led such a good life, and now he is going to have to die.' So a great wave of compassion came over him. He felt intensely sorry for the old monk, just sitting there and playing this game in obedience to the abbot's command, and now being beaten and soon to have to die. A tremendous compassion welled up in the young man's heart, and he thought, 'I can't allow this.' So he deliberately made a false move. The monk made a move. The young man deliberately made another false move, and it was clear that he was losing, and was unable to retrieve his position. But suddenly the abbot upset the board, saying, 'No one has won, and no one has lost.' Then to the young man he said, 'You have learned two things today: concentration and compassion. Since you have learned compassion—you'll do!'

Like the Mahāyāna sutras, this story teaches that all that is needed is compassion. The young man had led such a wretched, wasteful life, yet since he was capable of compassion there was still hope for him. He was even ready to give up his own life rather than let the monk sacrifice his—there was so much compassion deep down in the heart of this apparently worthless man. The abbot saw all this. He thought, 'We've got a budding Bodhisattva here,' and acted accordingly.

Muditā, *or Sympathetic Joy.*

Muditā, or sympathetic joy, is the happiness we feel in other people's happiness. If we see other people happy we should feel happy too; but unfortunately this is not always the case. A cynic has said that we feel a secret satisfaction in the misfortunes of our friends. This is often only too true. Next time someone tells you of a stroke of bad luck they have had, watch your own reaction. You will usually see, if only for an instant, a little quiver of satisfaction— after which of course the conventional reaction smothers your first *real* reaction. This secret joy in others' misfortune can be eliminated with the help of awareness, and also by means of a positive effort to share in other people's happiness.

Speaking generally, joy is a characteristically Buddhist emotion. If you are not happy and joyful, at least on some occasions, you can hardly be a Buddhist. In the East— though you might find this rather strange—there is no association of religion with gloom. In England, in the past at least, there was certainly a tendency to associate religion with gloom. People thought that the more serious and solemn and sad you looked, the more religious you were. If you went around happy and joyful, especially on the Sabbath, you were clearly an irreligious, impious, pagan sort of person. This may be an exaggeration, but I have heard that in the old days in Scotland you could be prosecuted for laughing on the Sabbath.

Unfortunately Buddhism in Britain has also been infected by these attitudes, especially in the past. I remember that the first time I attended a Wesak celebration in London I was appalled. People looked as though they had come to a funeral—probably their parents'! When in the course of my talk I made a few jokes and humorous references some of the audience looked quite startled. A few did venture to smile and even to laugh, but it was clear that they were not accustomed to that sort of thing. In my talk I even went so far as to say, 'This is very strange! I have celebrated Wesak all over the Buddhist world, in Ceylon, Singapore, Kalimpong, and Bombay, with Tibetans, Sikkimese, Sinhalese, Burmese, Chinese, Japanese, and Thais, and have always found them happy on Wesak day. But here everyone seems so sad, as though they were not happy that the Buddha had gained Enlightenment!' This was in 1965, and things have certainly altered for the better since then. At least Buddhists no longer celebrate Wesak as though it was a penance, but appreciate that it is an occasion for rejoicing. Indeed the whole Buddhist movement in Britain now presents a more cheerful and joyous aspect.

Upekṣā, *or tranquillity*
Upekṣā means tranquillity or, more simply, peace. We usually think of peace as something negative, as the absence of noise or disturbance, as when we say, 'I wish they would leave me in peace.' But really peace is a very positive thing. It is no less positive than love, compassion, or joy—indeed it is even more so, according to Buddhist tradition. *Upekṣā* is not simply the absence of something else, but a quality and a state in its own right. It is a positive, vibrant state which is much nearer to the state of bliss than it is to our usual conception of peace. Peace in this sense is also an important aspect of Perfect Emotion.

Śraddhā, *or faith and devotion*
Śraddhā is usually translated as faith, but it is not faith in the sense of belief. Rather it is the emotional aspect of our total response to the truth, especially the truth as embodied in certain symbols. In Buddhism faith and devotion are directed especially towards the Three Jewels, or Three Most Precious Things: The Buddha, the enlightened

teacher; the Dharma, or the teaching of the way to Enlightenment; and the Sangha, the community of disciples
treading the way to Enlightenment. These Three Jewels
have their appropriate symbols. The Buddha is symbol-
ized by the Buddha image, the Dharma or teaching by the
scriptures, and the Sangha by the members of the monastic
order. Throughout the Buddhist East, in all Buddhist
countries, these three symbols—the image, the scriptures,
and the monks—are treated with great reverence, not on
their own account, but because of what they represent and
symbolize.

The Sevenfold Puja
We have already seen that in Buddhism there are practices
for developing *maitrī*, or love. In the same way in Buddhism, as in other religions, there are practices for developing
faith and devotion. One such practice is called the *Sevenfold Puja*. As its name suggests this consists of seven parts,
representing a sequence of devotional moods and attitudes, accompanied where necessary with appropriate
ritual actions.

The first stage of the Sevenfold Puja is *pūjā*, or worship.
This consists in the making of offerings. In the simplest
form of *pūjā* the offerings consist simply of flowers, lights
—whether lighted candles or lamps—and burning in-
cense-sticks. There are also what are known as the seven
ordinary offerings, consisting of water for drinking, water
for washing the feet, flowers, incense, light, perfume, food,
and sometimes an eighth offering, music. These are, incidentally, the ancient Indian offerings to the honoured
guest.

Even today in India, if you visit anyone's house as an
honoured guest they will at once give you a glass of water
to drink, because it is very hot in India and you are likely
to be thirsty. You will then be given water for washing the

feet, and often your hosts will wash your feet themselves, especially if you are a monk, because you have come over the dusty roads of India and your feet are dusty. After that you are presented with a garland of flowers, and your hosts will light incense sticks to create a pleasant atmosphere and keep away flies and mosquitoes. If it is evening they will light a lamp. They will then offer perfume for the body, and, of course, something to eat. After the meal there will sometimes be a little music.

This is the way in which the honoured guest is entertained in India, and it was the seven or eight offerings to the honoured guest which became, in Buddhism, the seven or eight religious offerings. These offerings are made to the Buddha because he comes into the world as a guest, as it were, from a higher plane of existence. He represents the irruption into this mundane world of something Transcendental, so he is treated and honoured as a guest. Sometimes the seven or eight offerings are offered in kind, in which case you have actual water, flowers, incense, light, perfume, and food set out on the 'steps' of the shrine; but more often, especially among Tibetans, there are seven bowls of water instead.

The second stage of the Sevenfold Puja is *vandanā*, which means obeisance or salutation. This consists of paying respect with the body. Some people take the view that it is enough to *feel* respect and reverence for the Buddha. This may be true, but if you feel these emotions strongly enough you will want to express them externally. If you like someone you do not want to keep your feeling all in the mind. You express it externally, because you are a totality—not just mind, but speech and body too. Thus if you feel true veneration for the Buddha you will not want to keep it just in the mind: you will express it spontaneously with your body, in terms of physical action.

There are many different forms of *vandanā* or obeisance,

from simply joining the hands in salutation, as when we chant the Sevenfold Puja, to making a full prostration on the floor, which is done on ceremonial occasions. But whether we put the hands together, or just put the finger-tips together, or even go down on the floor full length, all these forms of obeisance represent a humble and receptive attitude on our part. They express our openness to the spiritual inspiration coming from the Buddha.

The third stage of the Sevenfold Puja is *Going for Refuge* to the Buddha, the Dharma, and the Sangha. This represents a commitment to the Buddha as our spiritual ideal, to the Dharma as the way to realize that ideal, and to the Sangha as the community of those in whose company we work towards that ideal. Going for Refuge marks a turning point in our spiritual life. It represents a total reorientation of our whole life in the direction of the ideal. Formal 'taking' of the refuges consists in repeating the formula of refuge, plus certain *śīlas*, or ethical precepts, after a monk. This makes one what is called an Upāsaka or Upasīkā, a lay brother or lay sister, which is the first level of the Buddhist Order.*

The Going for Refuge section of the Sevenfold Puja is followed by the *Confession of Faults*. Confession is of great importance in all forms of Buddhism, though its significance is psychological rather than theological. Many

---

*At this point in the original lecture, given during the first year of the Friends of the Western Buddhist Order's existence, Sangharakshita spoke of the possibility of Upāsaka and Upāsikā ordinations being held shortly under its auspices. The first of these ordinations took place on 7 April 1968, thus bringing into existence the Western Buddhist Order, which at the date of going to press in November 1990 numbered 416 ordained members. Since 1968 the requirements for ordination have been upgraded to such an extent that it is no longer possible to refer to members of the Order as Upāsakas and Upāsikās—lay brothers and lay sisters. They are now simply known as Dharmacāris and Dharmacāriṇīs, or 'Practisers of the Dharma', and there is only one level of ordination for all.

people suffer from repressed feelings of guilt, leading very often to self-hatred. They cannot develop *maitrī* or love, at least not in its fullness. Buddhist monks, if conscious of any fault or shortcoming, confess among themselves, especially to their own teachers, or to the Buddha. It is also the custom, if you are conscious of any fault or shortcoming in yourself, to burn incense in front of the image of the Buddha and recite sutras, and to go on doing this until you feel free from the sense of guilt. Although this is very important psychologically these practices do not absolve you from the consequences of the fault that has been committed. You still have to suffer the consequences of your actions, but you are free, subjectively, from the feeling of remorse or guilt. This is very important, because such feelings can poison or vitiate our whole spiritual life.

The fifth stage of the Sevenfold Puja is *Rejoicing in Merits*. This is complementary to the previous practice. If you think about your faults and contemplate your numerous backslidings too much or too often you may become a bit disheartened. So after confessing your faults you should inspire yourself by recollecting the virtues of others, thinking especially of the Buddhas and Bodhisattvas, of the lives they have led, and the perfections they have practised. Think, say, of the inspiring example of Milarepa, or Han Shan, or Hui Neng, or Hakuin. Or think of the various secular heroes and heroines who have lived for the benefit of others, and whose lives are an inspiration to us: people like Florence Nightingale and Elizabeth Fry, great humanitarians, great social reformers. Think, even, of the virtues of ordinary people: think of your own friends, how well they sometimes act, how unselfish they are on occasion, how kind. Dwell on this more positive side of their natures, and in this way learn to appreciate— to rejoice in—the merits of all other living beings, from the Buddhas and Bodhisattvas right down to the ordinary people who happen to be your friends and neighbours. This will give you a feeling of exhilaration, even of support. You will realize that you are not alone in the world, spiritually speaking, but are treading the same path that others trod, and *are* treading, successfully. On account of this realization you will feel buoyed up in your own spiritual life and spiritual endeavour.

The sixth stage, *Entreaty and Supplication*, is based on a legendary episode in the Buddha's life. According to the legend, after the Buddha's Enlightenment a certain deity, Brahmā Sahampati by name, appeared before him and requested him to make known the truth he had discovered, out of compassion for all living beings. We must understand the true significance of this story. It is not that the Buddha needed to be reminded of what he had to do. He did not need Brahmā Sahampati to come and advise him that he ought to teach. What this episode and this part of the Puja signifies is that the disciple must be ready: the disciple must really want the teaching and must entreat, as it were, the teacher, the Buddha, to give the teaching. 'When the disciple is ready the master will appear.' This part of the Puja, then, represents that readiness and willingness to receive the teaching.

The seventh and last stage of the Sevenfold Puja is *Transference of Merits and Self-Surrender*. This consists in wishing that whatever merit, whatever benefit, you might have gained from celebrating this Puja, or from performing any other religious act—whether observing the precepts, Going for Refuge, studying Buddhist philosophy, or practising meditation—can be shared with all other living beings. You are not concerned just with your own salvation. You have not got your eye on Nirvana for your own sake only. You want to gather up the whole of humanity, indeed all living beings, and help them as well as yourself—contribute to *their* evolution in the direction of the goal of Nirvana. There is no room for religious individualism in the spiritual life. When you practise any religious exercise you should feel that all other living beings are practising with you.

In the Mahāyāna there is a way of deliberately developing this attitude. When performing a religious exercise you visualize everybody else as doing it with you and sharing in its benefits. If you sit and meditate, think of everybody else meditating. When you chant the Buddha's praises, think of everybody else as chanting. When you recite a mantra, think of everybody else as reciting. In this way you develop the feeling of sharing whatever benefits you derive from your spiritual practice with other people. This feeling paves the way for taking what we call the Bodhisattva Vow: the vow that one will gain Enlightenment not for one's own sake only, but for the sake of all living beings whatsoever; that one will carry them with one, so that *all* gain Enlightenment, *all* enter Nirvana, *all* achieve Supreme Buddhahood.

This is the Sevenfold Puja: a very beautiful sequence of devotional moods to which we give expression in appropriate words and actions.

Most of the positive emotions I have referred to are what are called social emotions. They are emotions which refer to other people, and which arise in the course of our various relationships with others. We do not feel these emotions alone. They spring up between us and other people. They spring up within the group. The positive emotions—love, compassion, joy, and so on—are much more easily cultivated in the group, where people at least sometimes have friendly and happy faces. If we just sit at home trying to be loving and compassionate and joyous it will not be so easy. This is why we have a spiritual community, a Sangha, an Order—because it makes the transformation of our emotional nature so much easier to achieve. And unless we transform our emotional nature there is for us no spiritual life. This is why it is so important that in the group, in the community, in the Sangha, we cultivate all the time the right spirit. A spiritual community, we may say, is not really a spiritual community unless people are actually developing within it, and finding it easier to develop, the positive emotions of love, compassion, generosity, peace, faith, and devotion. It is for the sake of the development of such emotions, and the transformation of our emotional nature, that we have a spiritual community. If the spiritual community does not function in this way, then it is better not to have a group or community at all.

III *The Ideal of Human Communication*
Perfect Speech

We have seen that Perfect Vision—with the arising of which entry upon the Eightfold Path takes place—is not just an intellectual understanding of Buddhism, however clear and profound, but something much more than that. It consists in an actual insight into the true or ultimate nature of existence itself, and it is of the character of a spiritual experience. This experience may be momentary. It may come and go in a flash. But it is something much more real, much more direct, more intimate, more personal, more true, than any intellectual understanding. Perfect Vision is a glimpse—an experience—of ultimate reality, however brief, momentary, or evanescent this may be.

But a glimpse is not enough. It is not enough that a vision should arise and transfigure us for a moment. It has to descend into every aspect of our lives. It has to penetrate into every limb. It has not only to transfigure, but to transform, our entire being—at every level, in every aspect.

(This is, incidentally, the significance of what we call *mudrā* in Buddhism. A *mudrā* is a gesture made with the hand, or a certain position taken by the fingers. Often we speak in terms of *samādhi, mantra,* and *mudrā.* Here *samādhi* represents the inner spiritual realization, *mantra* the expression of that realization in terms of speech, while *mudrā* is the expression of that same realization to the very tips of one's fingers—to the outermost ramifications of one's being—in terms of gesture. *Mudrā* is sometimes translated as 'magic gesture', just as *maṇḍala* is sometimes translated as 'magic circle', but it is not anything magical at all. On the contrary, it is something spiritual, even transcendental.)

Our spiritual realization is not to be confined to the heights. It has to descend into the depths of our being and transform every aspect and department of our lives. When this happens, and our lives are transformed in every aspect, and at every level, in accordance with Perfect Vision—in accordance with our insight into, and experience of, the Truth—*then* comes what we call Enlightenment.

We have seen that Perfect Emotion, the second stage or aspect of the Path, represents the descent of Perfect Vision into our emotional life. It represents the transformation or sublimation of our crude, unrefined emotional energies into something much more delicate, much more rarified—something, if we may use the term, much more spiritual.

Now we come to the third aspect of the Buddha's Noble Eightfold Path, which is Right Speech—*samyag-vācā* in Sanskrit. In this case the translation presents no problems. Here there is no ambiguity, no nuance to be rendered with some difficulty into English. *Vācā* means simply speech or utterance in a quite literal sense, while *samyag* (or *samyak*), as in the case of the other stages of the Path, means not just right as opposed to wrong—the usual translation—but that which is whole, complete, integral, fully developed, perfect. We shall therefore speak of *samyag-vācā* in English not just as Right Speech, but as Perfect Speech. This is what it really means.

It is very significant that Perfect Speech is regarded as an independent stage or aspect of the Eightfold Path. One might have thought that speech was not so important, and that being a sort of action it could be included under Right Action, the next limb of the Eightfold Path. But that is not the case. In the Buddha's teaching as represented by the Eightfold Path, Perfect Speech gets a whole stage to itself. This indicates the very great importance Buddhism gives to speech in general, and especially to Perfect Speech. Not only is Perfect Speech the third aspect of the Buddha's Noble Eightfold Path, but abstention from its opposite—false or imperfect speech—constitutes the fourth of the five precepts every lay Buddhist is expected to observe.

Speech or verbal communication is something in which we have to engage all the time. You may take up meditation or not, as you wish; but when it comes to speech you have hardly any choice. Whether you like it or not you have to speak, you have to talk, you have to *communicate*. You cannot always be silent, even if you want to; and in any case most of us do not want to be silent—not very much of the time anyway. It is therefore inevitable that some consideration should be given to the question of speech in any systematic programme of spiritual training and culture. Speech has to be brought under the influence, even under the control, of the spiritual life. Hence it must be considered and given a place.

In the West man is usually regarded as consisting of body and mind, sometimes of body, soul, and spirit; but in Buddhism there is a threefold division of man into body, speech, and mind. It is one of those little things that are so ordinary we pass them over, but its significance is very great. It means that in Buddhism speech is given the same importance as mind, the same importance as body. Body, speech, and mind are a sort of co-equal trinity.

If we think about it, it is speech which distinguishes man from the beasts. We know that birds utter cries, some monkeys have a kind of primitive speech, and apparently dolphins can communicate. But speech in the full distinctive sense seems to be the prerogative of human beings; perhaps also of angels, but we have knowledge only of human beings. This speech is something special, something extraordinary, something which really does distinguish us from other forms of life. If we reflect we shall see that a great part of our culture depends, directly or indirectly, on speech. Through speech the mother and the teacher educate the child. Through books, which are, as it were, frozen, crystallized speech, we get information, we get knowledge; we may even get Enlightenment.

All our culture, all knowledge, even our spiritual insight, is to a great extent derived directly or indirectly from the *word*—from speech, from utterance. It is therefore natural, even inevitable, that in the moral and spiritual life we should give as much consideration to speech as we do to thought and action.

There are three great phases in the historical development of Buddhism: the Hinayāna, the Mahāyāna, and the Vajrayāna. In the Vajrayāna—the Adamantine Path or Way—body, speech, and mind are associated respectively with three psychic centres, as we may call them (without attaching too much importance to the word psychic). The body is associated with the head centre, speech with the throat centre, and mind with the heart centre. This is why when we salute the Buddha image, or our teacher, we often do this by joining our hands, and with them touching our head, throat, and chest in succession: to signify that we salute with body, speech, and mind, with our whole being, completely, fully, without holding anything back.

There are many other correlations of body, speech, and mind—for instance with the three *kāyas*, or 'personalities' of the Buddha—but this is not the place to go into them. At the moment we are concerned with just one point: that the throat centre, representing speech, lies between the head and the heart centres. The head, or head centre, represents not only body but also, in another set of correlations, the intellect or understanding; while the heart, or heart centre, represents the feelings and emotions. That speech, at the throat centre, lies in between, means that speech shares the nature of both. Speech gives expression both to the head and the heart. With speech we communicate both our thoughts and our emotions. As with ordinary speech, so also with Perfect Speech. Perfect Speech simultaneously represents or manifests Perfect Vision—which corresponds to intellectual understanding without being identical with it—and Perfect Emotion, which corresponds on its own plane to our emotional life. Very briefly and simply, through Perfect Speech we give expression both to wisdom and to love and compassion. In broad terms Perfect Speech represents the transformation of the speech principle, or principle of communication, by Perfect Vision and Perfect Emotion.

In Buddhist texts Perfect Speech is usually described as speech which is truthful, which is affectionate, which is helpful, and which promotes concord, harmony, and unity. Similarly wrong or imperfect speech is described in precisely opposite terms, as speech which is untruthful, harsh, harmful, and which promotes discord, disharmony, and disunity.

Most Buddhist expositions of Perfect Speech (or Right Speech, as it is usually termed), especially the modern ones, are rather superficial and moralistic. They remain on the purely ethical level, and usually no attempt is made to penetrate or explore the psychological and spiritual depths of Perfect Speech. In fact we may say that this is true of some people's approach to the whole teaching of the Buddha, and especially to the teaching of the Noble Eightfold Path. People are sometimes misled by the apparent simplicity of the Buddha's teaching, so that even when expounding it, or professing to expound it, they tend to dismiss it is something rather trite and ordinary. They do not try to penetrate below the surface and see what the Buddha was really getting at.

With regard to Perfect Speech, it is usually thought that truthfulness, affectionateness, helpfulness, and the promotion of concord, harmony, and unity, are four separate qualities or attributes of Perfect Speech, as though on the one hand we have Perfect Speech, and on the other these four attributes which are, as it were, stuck to it. But if we go a little more deeply and examine this aspect of the Eightfold Path more carefully, we shall discover that these four so-called qualities of Perfect Speech really represent four different levels of speech, each one deeper than the one preceding. We may even speak, in this connection, of four progressive levels of communication.

In the light of these considerations we are going to examine each of these four levels of Perfect Speech. This will give us at least a glimpse, at least some idea, not just of Right Speech, or even Perfect Speech, but of the ideal of human communication—what human communication should be or could be, according to the teaching of the Buddha. We shall perhaps see how far short we usually fall of this Perfect Speech, this ideal communication. We communicate, we talk, all the time. But practically all the time, if not always, we fall short of this ideal. Let us try to see what, according to the Buddha's teaching, this Perfect Speech or ideal of human communication really is.

1. The level of truthfulness

First of all Perfect Speech, or ideal communication, is truthful. We all think we know exactly what is meant when it is said that all speech should be truthful. We have been told since we were two years old not to tell a lie, like George Washington. But do we really know what is meant by speaking the truth? Have we considered all the implications? Speaking the truth does not mean just adhering to factual accuracy, saying that this cloth is yellow and that *that* is a microphone. The concept of truthfulness is not exhausted in this way. Factual accuracy is of course important. It is one of the elements of truthfulness, and we cannot dismiss it. But it is not the whole.

Those of you who know your Boswell will remember the famous remark of Dr Johnson about factual truthfulness. He remarks that if your children say that something happened at one window, when in fact it happened at another, then they should be instantly checked, because once it begins you do not know where deviation from the truth will end. Thus factual truthfulness is important. It is the basis or foundation of Perfect Speech. Recognizing this, we should accustom ourselves to what Johnson calls 'accuracy of narration', which is a sort of training ground for us in the higher, more refined kinds of truthfulness. Usually we are shaky and shoddy even on this level. Few people really practise accuracy of narration. We usually like to make things a little bit different. We like to pad out, we like to exaggerate, or to minimize, or to embroider. It may just be a poetic streak in us which makes us do this, but we do it even in the best of circles, even at the best of times.

In this connection I remember once attending a little Wesak celebration at a certain Buddhist centre in India. There must have been seventy or eighty people present, but the write-up I saw later in a Buddhist magazine spoke of a 'mammoth meeting' attended by thousands of people. The writer might have thought he was propagating the Dharma and stirring up faith and enthusiasm in this way, but really he was detracting from what he was supposed to be doing. He was not being truthful in the sense of being factually accurate.

We all tend to twist, or distort, or at least slightly bend facts, in the direction in which we would like them to go, so we have to be extremely careful here. If we say for instance that it was a lovely day, it must have been a lovely day. We must neither exaggerate nor minimize. If we say that there were ten people at the meeting, let us be sure that there were ten. If there were a thousand, let us say that there were a thousand. But if there were only fifty, let us not make it one-hundred-and-fifty. Or in the case of somebody else's meeting, if there were a thousand, let us not make it one-hundred-and-fifty! Thus we must pay strict attention to factual accuracy, though it must again be emphasized that truthfulness in the real sense, in the deepest, the fullest, the most spiritual sense, is something very much more than mere factual accuracy, important as this is.

Truthfulness is also psychological, also spiritual. Besides factual accuracy speaking the truth also involves an attitude of honesty and sincerity. It involves saying what we *really* think. You are not speaking the truth unless you speak the whole truth, and say what is really in your heart and mind—say what you really think, even what you really feel. If you do not do that you are not being truthful, you are not really communicating.

But then another question arises: do we really even know what we think? Do we really know what we feel? Most of us live or exist in a state of chronic mental confusion, bewilderment, chaos, disorder. We may repeat, as the occasion arises, what we have heard, what we have read. We may regurgitate it when we are required to do so, whether at the time of examinations in the case of students, or on social occasions in the case of other people. But we do all this without really knowing what we say. How can we, therefore, really speak the truth? Since we do not really know what we think, how can we be truthful?

If we want to speak the truth in the full sense, or at least in a fuller sense than is usually understood, we must clarify our ideas. We must introduce some sort of order into this intellectual chaos of ours. We must know quite clearly, quite definitely, what we think, what we do not think, what we feel, what we do not feel. And we must be intensely aware. We must know what is within us, what are our motivations, what are our drives and our ideals. This means that we have to be completely honest with ourselves. It means that we have to know ourselves. If we do not know ourselves, in the depths as well as on the heights, if we cannot penetrate into the depths of our own being and be really transparent to ourselves, if there is not any clarity or illumination within—then we cannot speak the truth.

This is something we all have to realize. If we do realize it we shall see that speaking the truth is no easy matter. We might even go so far as to say—and I do not think this is an exaggeration—that most of us, most of the time, do not speak the truth. If we wanted to put it forcibly, not to say paradoxically, we might even say that most of us, nearly all the time, speak what is in fact a lie, and that our communication is in fact most of the time a lie, because we are not capable of speaking anything else. We are incapable of speaking the truth in the fullest sense. If we reflect we might have to admit that most of us go through life, year after year, from childhood or at least adolescence into old age, without perhaps being able even once to speak the truth in the fullest and clearest sense of that much abused term.

We do know that if ever we are in a position to speak the truth, then it is a great relief to be able to do so. Often we do not realize how many lies we have been telling until we have an opportunity, once in a while perhaps, of speaking the truth. We all know that if something has been weighing on our mind or on our heart, something about which we were very worried or concerned, if we can only speak out—or tell somebody the truth of the matter, without holding back—then it is a great relief. Unfortunately for most people this is something that happens very rarely in their lives, if indeed at all.

Speaking the truth really means being ourselves. Not in the conventional, social sense, as when we are said to 'be ourselves' at a party, which usually means not being ourselves at all; but in the sense of giving expression in terms of speech to what we really and truly are and know we are. Speaking the truth, however, even in this more rarified, fuller, deeper and more spiritual sense, is not done in a vacuum. You do not just go up to the top of the Post Office Tower and speak the truth to the stars. The truth is always spoken to someone—another person, another human being. This brings us to the second level of Perfect Speech, or the second stage of communication.

2. The level of affectionateness

Perfect Speech is not only truthful, even in the fullest sense; it is also affectionate and loving. It is the truth spoken in or with love. This does not mean just using terms of endearment, or anything of that sort. Speaking with affection or love in this context means speaking the truth in its fullness, with complete awareness of the person to whom you are speaking. How many of us can do this? If we think about it we will realize that when we speak to people we do not usually look at them. Have you ever noticed this? It is probably true in your case, and in the case of people who speak to you. When they speak to you, or when you speak to them, you do not look at them. You look over their shoulder, you look at their forehead, up at the ceiling, down at the ground—anywhere, almost, except at the person to whom you are speaking. If you do not look at others (and this is one of the things we try to correct in our communication exercises, as some of you will know to your cost!) you cannot be aware of them.

We can say that love, in the sense in which we are using the term at present, means awareness of the being of another person. If, then, you do not *know* the other person, how can you speak affectionately to them? It just is not possible. We like to think, of course, that we have love for people, that we are affectionate, but this is very rarely so. We usually see other people in terms of our own emotional reactions to them. We react emotionally to them in a certain way, and then we attribute that emotional reaction *to* them as a quality *of* them. If for instance people do what we would like them to do, then we say that they are good, kind, helpful, and so on. Thus we are not really communicating with that particular person. What really happens, most of the time, is that we are communicating, or trying to communicate, or pretending to communicate, with our own mental projections.

This is especially so in the case of those who are—allegedly—near and dear to us. Parents and children, brothers and sisters, husbands and wives, very rarely know one another. They might have lived together for twenty, or thirty, or forty years, but they do not know one another. They know their own reactions to one another, and those reactions they attribute to the other person. They think, therefore, that they know them; but they do not really know them at all. They know only their own projected mental and emotional states.

This is a sobering thought. There used to be a saying, 'It is a wise father that knows his own child.' Well, it is a wise child that knows his own father; it is a wise wife that knows her own husband; it is a very wise husband that knows his own wife: because the more you live with people, especially those to whom you are related by blood or by strong emotional ties, the less, in the real spiritual sense, do you know them. After all, to the baby, what is mother? Mother is just a wonderful sensation of warmth and comfort, security and well-being: *that* is what mother is. The child does not know mother as a person. The same is true with other relations. And it usually remains like that for most of our lives, with a bit of refinement and rationalization here and there. This is true for most of us, most of the time.

This is why there is so much misunderstanding between people, so much failure to communicate, so many disappointments, especially in the more intimate relationships of life. People are at cross purposes because one person does not know another and therefore cannot love another. There is just pseudo-communication between projections, and nothing more. I know this sounds drastic and perhaps rather horrifying, but it is true; and I think it is best and most salutary if we face up to the truth about ourselves and other people as quickly as possible, and realize that, in most cases, our so-called relationships are just a maze of such mutual projections, with no mutual knowledge and understanding at all—not to speak of mutual love.

But if there *is* such a thing as mutual awareness and mutual love, and if we *are* able to speak the truth to another person, being aware of that other person—which means, of course, loving that other person, love being awareness of their being—we shall also know what they need. If we really know the other person we shall know what they need—as distinct from what we think they ought to have because it would be good for us if they had it, which is what most people mean by 'knowing what is good for others.' Knowing what people need means knowing what is good for them quite objectively, without reference to ourselves. We will then know what has to be provided, what given, how they have to be helped, and so on. This brings us to the third level of Perfect Speech, or the third stage of communication.

3. The level of helpfulness

According to the Buddha we should speak that which is useful, in the sense of speaking in such a way as to promote the growth, especially the spiritual growth, of the person to whom we are speaking. This need not involve anything as formal as specifically religious instruction, although this too is very useful. Broadly speaking this aspect of Perfect Speech—speaking that which is useful—consists in speaking in such a way that the person or persons to whom we are speaking are raised in the scale of being and consciousness, and not lowered. At least we can be positive and appreciative. Most people are so negative. You tell them about something good, something happy, and they either pull a long face, or depreciate it, or try to undermine you. In the end you may feel quite guilty about having enjoyed that particular thing, or having liked and appreciated it. So we must at least be positive and appreciative, realizing that when we have this kind of attitude the other person is helped to grow—not when we are negative, critical, or destructive.*

There is a beautiful story which illustrates this point, taken from one of the apocryphal gospels. (In the early days of Christianity, there were not just the four gospels found in the Bible, but scores, even hundreds, of gospels. Some of these have come down to us, and contain sayings and anecdotes not found in the Bible.) According to this story, Jesus was walking along the road with his disciples, somewhere in Galilee, when they came upon a dead dog.

---

* Constructive criticism, based on emotional positivity and genuine concern for the other person, is not of course excluded. Such criticism —which may be mutual—promotes spiritual growth. It is therefore useful in the best sense of the term, and to be included under Perfect Speech.

We do not usually see dead dogs in the streets of London, but in the East it is a common sight even now, and as those of you who have read Baudelaire's famous poem will realize, a dead dog is not a pretty sight. That particular dog must have lain there for several weeks, for when they came upon it the disciples reacted with expressions of disgust and horror. Jesus, however, smiled and said, 'What beautiful teeth!' He saw what was beautiful even in a dead dog.

This is the sort of attitude which this level of Perfect Speech requires. We should see the good, the bright, the positive side of things—not fasten our attention on the negative. We should not be over-critical or destructive. There is a time of course for criticism, even destructive criticism: that is a legitimate activity. But most of us take to it far too readily and easily, to the neglect of the more positive side. Even if we are not in a position to give specifically spiritual instruction, or to enlighten people— and very few of us can do that in any way, or to any extent—we can at least be helpful. We can at least be positive, and appreciative of whatever good we see growing in, or emerging from, that other person. In any case even if we do on occasion give some sort of instruction, this will only be effective if given in a helpful, positive, and constructive spirit.

Now if we communicate in the way we have described: if we speak the truth, the whole truth, and nothing but the truth; if we speak with love, that is with awareness of the other person's being; if we speak in such a way as to promote the other's growth, to have a healthy, positive effect on them; if we are more concerned about their needs than about our own; if we are not projecting our own emotional states, or using or exploiting them; then the result will be that in speaking to, or communicating with, another person we will forget all about ourselves. This brings us to the fourth and highest level of Perfect Speech, or the fourth and final stage of communication.

4. The level of promoting concord, harmony, and unity

As well as all the qualities we have already described, Perfect Speech is speech which promotes concord, harmony, and unity. This does not just mean verbal agreement. It does not mean saying 'Yes, yes' all the time. It does not even mean sharing the same ideas—it is not a matter of 'You believe in Buddhism, I believe in Buddhism.' This is not what is meant here. What 'speech which promotes concord, harmony, and unity' really means is mutual helpfulness, based on truthfulness and awareness of each other's being and each other's needs, leading to mutual self-transcendence. This mutual self-transcendence is Perfect Speech *par excellence*. It is not only Perfect Speech, but also the perfection of communication. When this sort of concord, harmony, and unity, this sort of understanding, is complete, is perfect, nothing more need be said. Even on the ordinary level, when you get to know someone for the first time, for a while you do a lot of talking, exchange ideas, get to know one another; but the more you get to know each another, in a sense the less there is to say. When Perfect Speech culminates in harmony, in oneness and mutual self-transcendence, at the same time it also culminates in silence.

What the Buddha calls Perfect Speech represents the principle of communication in its highest form; but we should not therefore think that speech, even Perfect Speech, is the only vehicle of communication. In the Vajra-yāna form of Buddhism—the Buddhism of the Adamantine Path or Way—there are distinguished three levels of transmission of the Buddha's teaching. The first, or lowest, is the verbal. On this level the teaching—the spiritual experience—is transmitted by means of the spoken or written word. The next level is transmission through signs or symbols, as in the Zen story of the Buddha holding up a golden flower in the midst of the assembly. This was a sign. It had a meaning that only Mahākāśyapa understood; and through this sign, or through the meaning of this sign, the essence of the Buddha's spiritual experience was transmitted to Mahākāśyapa, and from him down a whole line of Zen masters. But according to the Vajrayāna the highest level of transmission is telepathic communication, which of course takes place in silence. This is the direct communication of mind with mind, without the interposition of either the spoken or written word, or the visual sign or symbol. It is mind flashing not signals, but itself, directly to another mind without any intermediary, without any medium of transmission at all. It is the direct, immediate impingement of mind on mind.

We should not think that silence is mere absence of sound. When all sound dies away—when the sound of the traffic in the street or the creaking of the chairs in the room, the sound of our own breath, and even the 'sound' of our thoughts, is utterly stilled—what is left is not just something negative or dead, not just a vacuum. What is left is a living silence.

In this connection I remember the very great example of the Indian sage and teacher Ramana Maharshi, who died in 1950. I had the good fortune to be with him for some time, about a year before he died, and he perfectly exemplified this attitude. He just sat there on a dais in the hall of the ashram, on a kind of settee with a tiger skin spread on it, and most of the time he said nothing at all. He had sat there for forty years, I think, and though the hall was usually full of people, when you entered there was a strangely vibrant quality to that silence. It quite literally seemed as though the silence flowed from him. You could almost see waves of silence flowing from him, flowing over all those people, flowing into their hearts and minds and calming them down. As you sat down yourself you quite literally felt the silence flowing over you, calming and quieting you, washing away all your thoughts. I am not speaking poetically or imaginatively—you felt it quite literally. You felt it as a sort of positive wave-like power flowing over you all the time. *This* was the silence— the real silence, the true silence—that Ramana Maharshi so beautifully exemplified.

Silence of this quality is very rare. Even ordinary silence, the lowest form of silence, is only too rare in modern life. Certainly in most of our lives there is far too much noise, and usually far too much talking. By talking I do not mean real communication through speech, but mere verbalization, the multiplication of words without too much meaning. One cannot help thinking that speech, which is so precious and so wonderful, so expressive and such a treasure, should be something exceptional. At least it should be something, like eating, that you do occasionally, after thought and preparation; but all too often speech precedes thought, while talking is the rule, and silence the exception.

But perhaps there is hope for us all, as there was for the young Macaulay, about whom the great wit Sydney Smith remarked, 'Macaulay is improving. He has flashes of silence'. Most of us are in this position. Maybe we *are* improving. Maybe we *do* have, occasionally, even quite brilliant flashes of silence. We should therefore perhaps try to make more time for silence in our lives: make more time just to be quiet, just to be alone, by ourselves. Unless we do this from time to time, say at least for an hour or two every day, we shall find the practice of meditation rather difficult.

We have apparently strayed a long way from Perfect Speech, and it might seem paradoxical that one should *speak*—especially at such length—in praise of silence. It is rather like that famous description of Carlyle's works: 'The Gospel of Silence, in forty volumes, by Mr Wordy'. Therefore I had perhaps better conclude with the hope that it is now obvious that much more is involved in Perfect Speech than at first might appear. Perfect Speech is not just Right Speech in the ordinary sense. It is the Buddha's ideal of human communication: perfectly truthful, in the fullest sense; perfectly affectionate; perfectly helpful; and perfectly promoting concord, harmony, and unity—or perfectly self-transcendent.

IV *The Principles of Ethics*
Perfect Action

With the fourth stage of the Noble Eightfold Path we come from Perfect Speech to Perfect Action, *samyak-karmānta* (Pali *sammā-kammanta*). This is the third stage of the Path of Transformation, and represents the descent into, and transformation of, all one's activities by Perfect Vision. *Karmānta* means action in the literal sense, so no lengthy explanations of the meaning of the term are required; while *samyak*, as has already been insisted, means whole, integral, complete, perfect. One should therefore speak not simply of Right Action but rather of Perfect Action.

The question of what constitutes Perfect Action is an important one, bringing us as it does straight to the heart of ethics, and compelling us to enquire into the fundamental principles of the subject. What is it that makes some acts right? What is it that makes others wrong? Is there any universally valid criterion in the light of which we can say that *this* is right and *that* is wrong, *this* is perfect and *that* imperfect? If there is any such criterion, where is it to be found? What is its nature? These are pressing and urgent questions that concern us all. Whether we like it or not we all have to act every day, every hour—almost every minute. The question of how to act in the best way, of what should be the criterion, the guiding principle or motive of our action, therefore inevitably arises.

The 'decline of morals'

Churchmen and others are fond of lamenting what they call the decline of morals. In the course of the last few decades everybody is supposed to have become progressively more immoral, and I gather we are now in a pretty bad state. The decline of morals is usually linked very firmly with the decline of religion, especially orthodox religion. Having turned our back on the Church, we are told, we have at once plunged into the pit, the mire, of immorality. Indeed we may argue that traditional ethics have to a very great extent collapsed. Many people are no longer convinced that there are any fixed standards of right and wrong. In the seventeenth century one of the Cambridge Platonists, Ralph Cudworth, wrote a book which he called *A Treatise on Eternal and Immutable Morality*. If anyone, even the Archbishop of Canterbury or the Pope, were to write a book with this title nowadays it would seem quite ridiculous. Even the great humanists and freethinkers of the nineteenth century, widely as they might range in their intellectual questioning, continued to conform to Christian ethics. Apart from one or two slips, when it came to their 'home life', as the Victorians called it, people like Darwin, Huxley, or even Marx, were models of morality. But that is all changed now. A young lady said to me the other day, 'If you do something and it makes you feel good, then that thing is right, at least for you.' This is a very widely held view. It may not always be held as explicitly, openly, and frankly as this; but it is, in fact, what many people think.

This development is not necessarily a bad thing. In the long run it might even be a good thing that morals should be thrown—temporarily we hope—into the melting-pot, and that we should have to re-think and re-feel, even re-imagine, our morality. It is good that, ultimately, as I hope, a new ethic should emerge from the ruins of the old.

Judaeo-Christian ethics

In retrospect it seems that Western ethics started off rather on the wrong foot. Our ethical tradition is a very composite thing. There are elements deriving from the classical Greek and Roman tradition; there are Judeo-Christian elements; and, especially in some of the northern European countries, there are elements of Germanic paganism. But though our Western ethical tradition is made up of many interwoven strands, it is the Judaeo-Christian element which predominates. This is the 'official' ethic to which, at least in the past, everybody paid lip-service, whatever their private practice or preference may have been.

In this Judaeo-Christian ethic morality is traditionally conceived very much in terms of Law. A moral obligation or moral rule is something laid upon man by God. This is well illustrated by the biblical account of the origin of the Ten Commandments. Moses goes up Mount Sinai and there, amidst thunder and lightning, he receives the Ten Commandments from God. On coming down from Mount Sinai with—according to Christian art—the two stone tablets on which they were inscribed tucked under his arm like a couple of tombstones, Moses in turn gives the Ten Commandments to the Children of Israel. This illustrates the idea of ethics as something imposed on man, almost against his will, by a power or authority external to himself. According to the Old Testament God has created man, has formed him out of the dust of the earth and breathed life into his nostrils. So man is God's creature, almost God's slave, and his duty is to obey. To disobey is a sin.

This attitude is again illustrated by the story of the Fall. Adam and Eve were punished, as we all know, for disobeying an apparently arbitrary order. God said, '... of the tree of knowledge of good and evil, thou shalt not eat.' But he did not give them any reason for the prohibition.

Nowadays we know that stories of this sort are mythical, but though few people any longer believe them to be literally true the attitudes which they represent still persist. The word *commandment* itself is significant. It is significant that a moral law or rule should be a *commandment* —something you are commanded to do, obliged to do, almost coerced into doing, by some power or authority external to yourself.

The two illustrations I have given are both from the Old Testament, and Christianity certainly goes beyond this conception of ethics; but it does not go very far beyond it, and even then only in a rather imperfect manner. The sources of specifically Christian ethics are, of course, to be found in Jesus's teaching as contained in the four Gospels; but according to Christian tradition Jesus is God, so when God himself tells you to do something the order obviously comes with a tremendous weight of authority behind it. Thus one does something not so much because it is good to do it but because one is asked to do it, even commanded to do it, by one in whom reposes all power and all authority in heaven and upon earth. Even within the context of Christian ethics, therefore, there is, generally speaking, this same idea of ethics as something obligatory, as something imposed upon one from without to which one must conform. This is our traditional heritage. This is the mode of thought by which, consciously or unconsciously, we are all influenced when we think in terms of ethics.

Nowadays the majority of people in Britain are not Christian in any meaningful sense, but nevertheless they still tend to think of morality, of ethics, in this way: as an obligation laid upon them from without, a command which they are obliged to obey. We can perhaps summarize the position of traditional ethics today by saying that it consists in not doing what we want to do, and doing what we do not want to do, because—for reasons we do not understand—we have been told to by someone in whose existence we no longer believe. So no wonder we are confused. No wonder we have no ethical signposts, and therefore have to try, in typically British fashion, to muddle through somehow or other. But though we try to make some sort of sense of our lives, try to discover some sort of pattern in events, where ethics is concerned the picture is mostly one of chaos.

The Buddhist criterion

Now I do not want to exaggerate, or to make the contrast seem too abrupt or dramatic, as between black and white, but in the Buddhist tradition the attitude to ethics is quite different from the one I have described. In fact this is true of the whole Eastern, especially Far Eastern, tradition. According to the Buddha's teaching, as preserved in the traditions of whatsoever sect or school, actions are right or wrong, perfect or imperfect, according to the state of mind with which they are performed. In other words the criterion of ethics is not theological but psychological. It is true that in the West we are not unacquainted with this idea, even within the context of Christianity; but so far as Buddhist ethics is concerned—indeed so far as Far Eastern ethics is concerned, whether Buddhist, Taoist, or Confucian—this criterion is the only one. It is a criterion which is universally applied and rigorously carried through to the very end.

According to Buddhist tradition there are two kinds of action, skilful (Skt *kauśalya*, Pali *kusala*) and unskilful (Skt *akauśalya*, Pali *akusala*). This is significant, because the terms skilful and unskilful, unlike the terms good and bad, suggest that morality is very much a matter of intelligence. You cannot be skilful unless you can understand things, unless you can see possibilities and explore them. Hence morality, according to Buddhism, is as much a matter of intelligence and insight as one of good intentions and good feelings. After all, we have been told that the path to hell is paved with good intentions; but you could hardly say that the path to hell is paved with skilfulness.

Unskilful actions are defined as those which are rooted in craving or selfish desire; in hatred or aversion; and in mental confusion, bewilderment, spiritual obfuscation, or ignorance. Skilful actions are those which are free from craving, free from hatred, free from mental confusion; positively speaking they are motivated instead by generosity, or the impulse to share and to give, by love and compassion, and by understanding. This very simple distinction at once places the whole question of morality in a very different light. The moral life becomes a question of acting from what is best within us: acting from our deepest understanding and insight, our widest and most comprehensive love and compassion.

We are now in a position to begin to see what is meant by Perfect Action. This is not just action which accords with some external standard or criterion, but action which expresses Perfect Vision and Perfect Emotion. Perfect Action represents the descent to the level of action of Perfect Vision and Perfect Emotion, just as Perfect Speech represents their descent to the level of communication. In other words, having already attained Perfect Vision and developed Perfect Emotion, when one comes to act one spontaneously expresses that vision and that emotional experience in terms of one's action.

Patterns of ethical behaviour
By this time serious students of Buddhism may well be wondering how the Five or the Ten *Śīlas* (Pali *Sīlas*) or Precepts fit into the picture. Are these not lists of moral rules which have been laid down by the Buddha himself,

and to which we must conform? In reply it may be said that while the *Śīlas* or sets of Precepts have certainly been taught, certainly been recommended, by the Buddha, they have not been laid down authoritatively, as the Ten Commandments were by God. What the Buddha says, in effect, is that one who is Enlightened, or who has attained Buddhahood, thereby realizing the plenitude of wisdom and the fullness of compassion, will inevitably behave in a certain way, because it is in the nature of an Enlightened being to behave in that way. Furthermore, to the extent that *you* are Enlightened, to that extent you *also* will behave in that way. If you are *not* Enlightened, or to the extent that you are not Enlightened, then the observance of the *Śīlas* or Precepts will help you to experience for yourself the state of mind of which they are, normally, the expression.

An example may make this point clear. We say that an Enlightened person, one who is a Buddha, is free from (let us say) craving or selfish desire. We ourselves are full of craving. We crave, for example, food of various kinds; we have a special liking for this or that. Suppose, as an experiment, we stop eating one of our favourite foodstuffs, whatever it may be. We give it up. We decide not to take it any more. Very regretfully, very sorrowfully, we close the larder door. We resist the temptation, whatever it may be—say plum cake. (I knew a Buddhist monk who was wonderfully addicted to plum cake. It was said you could get anything out of him if you offered him sufficient plum cake!) What happens is that we may suffer for a while, and may not have an easy time at all. In fact, it may be quite hard going. But if we stick it out, if we banish those visions of plum cake, craving is gradually reduced and eventually we shall reach a happy state where there is no craving at all, and where we never even think of that particular thing. Our abstention from plum cake is now no longer a disciplinary measure, but has become a genuine expression of the state of non-craving to which we have attained.

The *Śīlas* or Precepts are not just lists of rules, though when you come across them in books on Buddhism they may indeed read like that. Only too often the Buddha is represented as telling people all the things they should *not* do, and the impression is created that Buddhism is a very dreary and negative business. But the *Śīlas* are, in reality, just patterns of ethical behaviour. They are the natural expression of certain skilful mental states. Since they are the natural expression of skilful mental states, we can find out to what extent we have developed those states by checking our behaviour against the *Śīlas*. Let us take a quick look, therefore, at just a few of these *Śīlas* or patterns of ethical behaviour. As lists of rules they will be familiar to many, so we need not spend too much time on them. In any case we do not want to identify Perfect Action too closely with any of its specific expressions, however worthy and noble they may be.

First, however, let me make one observation. Different people's patterns of external ethical behaviour may be identical, but the mental states behind their behaviour may be quite different. This may sound a little complicated, but it is really very simple. Suppose, for example, that three different people abstain from theft. The first person would like to steal, perhaps very much, but he abstains out of fear of the police. (This is the morality of many people.) The second person has a slight inclination towards dishonesty. When filling in his income tax return he may be seriously tempted to cheat, but because he is trying to lead a spiritual life he resists the temptation. The inclination is there, but it is restrained. However the third person has completely eradicated craving. In his case there is no tendency, no inclination towards dishonesty. The first person, who abstains from theft through fear of the police, is moral only in the legalistic sense. The second person, who feels an inclination to steal and overcomes it, is moral in the sense that he is practising Right Action in the narrower, 'disciplinary' sense. Only the third, who abstains because it is natural for him to do so, is really practising Perfect Action.

The Five *Śīlas* and the Five *Dharmas*

The best known pattern of ethical behaviour is that of the Five *Śīlas*, generally known as the Five Precepts. The Five Precepts, as usually transmitted, are negative in form. They tell us what *not* to do. In the case of each Precept, however, there is a positive counterpart. It is very significant that in modern Buddhist teaching the positive counterpart is far less widely known than the negative formulation. Many people will have heard of the Five *Śīlas* who have not heard of the Five *Dharmas*, as the five positive counterparts are called. In this context, the Five *Dharmas* may be translated as the Five Ethical Principles. We shall briefly consider both the Five Precepts and the Five *Dharmas*, one by one, examining first the negative and then the positive formulation. This will give us a balanced picture of this particular pattern of Buddhist ethics.

The first of the Five Precepts is *abstention from harming living beings*. This is the literal translation. Although sometimes rendered as 'not to kill', it is really abstention not only from killing but from harming in any way. It conveys the meaning of abstention from all forms of violence, all forms of oppression, all forms of injury. Violence is wrong because ultimately it is based, directly or indirectly, on an unskilful mental state—on the state of hatred or aversion —and if we indulge in violence this unskilful mental state, of which violence is the natural expression, will become stronger and more powerful than it is already.

The positive counterpart of abstention from violence is the practice of *maitrī* (Pali *mettā*): love or friendliness. Here *maitrī* is not just an emotion or a feeling, but is embodied in deeds and put into practice. It is not enough simply to *feel* goodwill towards others. This feeling must be expressed in action. Otherwise, if we simply gloat over it in our own mind, thinking how much we love everybody and how kind we are, it becomes a sort of emotional self-indulgence—not to say something worse. So we should watch ourselves in this respect. We often consider we love other people. At least, we consider we love *some* other people. But if we examine ourselves, we find that we never really express our love: we take it for granted that it is understood.

A familiar example is that of the couple who have been married for twenty or thirty years, and the husband never bothers to bring the wife as much as a bunch of flowers or a box of chocolates. If someone were to ask him, 'Don't you love your wife? You never take her as much as a bunch of flowers or a box of chocolates,' the average husband would reply, 'What's the need? Of course I love her, but she should know that after all these years!' This is very bad psychology. People should not have to take it for granted, or just imagine, that we do have feelings towards them. It should be quite obvious from our words and actions. Indeed we should actually take steps to keep alive the spirit of love and friendship. That is why in all social life, and in Buddhist social life especially, such things as exchanging gifts and extending invitations are very much emphasized. It is not enough to sit in your own room, or even in your own cell, radiating thoughts of love. Good and wonderful though that may be, it must come down to some concrete expression. Only then will such thoughts be reciprocated in a tangible way by other people.

The second of the Five Precepts is *abstention from taking the not-given*. This, again, is a literal translation. It is not just abstention from theft. That would be too easy to evade or to circumvent. The second Precept involves abstention from any kind of dishonesty, any kind of misappropriation or exploitation, because all these are expressions of craving, or selfish desire. The positive counterpart of abstention from taking the not-given is *dāna*, or generosity. Here again it is not simply the generous feeling, the will to give, that is meant, but the generous act itself. There is no need for me to elaborate. *Dāna* is something which all those who have contact with living Buddhism for any length of time very quickly come to understand.

The third Precept is *abstention from sexual misconduct*. In the sutras the Buddha makes it clear that in the context of the Five Precepts sexual misconduct comprises rape, abduction, and adultery. All three are unskilful because they are expressions, simultaneously, of both craving and violence. In the case of rape and abduction, which in the comparatively unorganized society of the Buddha's day seem to have been fairly common, violence is committed against the woman herself, and also, if she happens to be a minor, against her parents or guardians. In the case of adultery, the violence is committed against the person's usual sexual partner, inasmuch as their domestic life is deliberately disrupted. It should be noted at this point that in Buddhism marriage is a purely civil contract, not a sacrament. Moreover, divorce is permitted, and from a religious point of view monogamy is not compulsory. In some parts of the Buddhist world there are communities which practise polygamy, and this is not considered sexual misconduct.

The positive counterpart of abstention from sexual misconduct is *saṁtuṣṭi* (Pali *santuṭṭhi*), or contentment. In the case of the unmarried, contentment means contentment with the single state. In the case of the married it means contentment with one's recognized, socially accepted sexual partner(s). Here contentment is not just passive acceptance of the status quo. In modern psychological terms, it means a positive state of freedom from using sex to satisfy neurotic needs in general and, in particular, using it to satisfy the neurotic need for change.

The fourth Precept is *abstention from false speech.* False speech is speech which is rooted in craving, hatred, or fear. If you tell a lie, it is either because you want something, or because you wish to harm or hurt someone, or because for one reason or another you are afraid of telling the truth. Untruthfulness, therefore, is rooted in unskilful mental states. This requires no demonstration. The positive counterpart of abstention from false speech is *satya* (Pali *sacca*), or truthfulness, which has already been discussed in connection with Perfect Speech.

The last of the Five Precepts is *abstention from drink and drugs the taking of which results in loss of awareness.* There is a certain amount of disagreement about the interpretation of this precept. In some Buddhist countries it is interpreted as requiring strict teetotalism, that is, total abstinence; in other Buddhist countries it is interpreted as requiring moderation in the use of anything which, taken in excess, is likely to result in intoxication. So one is free to take one's choice between these two interpretations. The positive counterpart of the precept is *smrti* (Pali *sati*): mindfulness or awareness. This is the real criterion. If you can drink without impairing your mindfulness (it might be said), then drink; but if you can't, then don't. However one must be quite honest with oneself, and not pretend that one is mindful when one is merely merry. Thus, even if the fifth Precept is interpreted as requiring simply moderation, in the light of its positive counterpart total abstinence will still be required in the vast majority of cases.

Such are the Five Precepts and the Five Principles, which are a very well known and widely accepted pattern of Buddhist morality or ethics. Two other patterns may also be mentioned.

The Bhikṣu Saṁvara-śīla *and Bodhisattva* Saṁvara-śīla

The Bhikṣu *Saṁvara-śīla* (Pali Bhikkhu *Saṁvara-sīla*) comprises the one-hundred-and-fifty precepts observed by the fully ordained monk, and represents the natural pattern of behaviour of one who is fully dedicated to the attainment of Nirvana. In other words, if we think of nothing but Nirvana and the attainment of Nirvana, devoting all our time and energy to following the spiritual path, our pattern of behaviour will approximate, quite naturally, to the pattern embodied in this list of a hundred-and-fifty-precepts. Unfortunately, these hundred-and-fifty precepts are all too often regarded as a list of rules, and thus the whole spirit behind them is lost.

The Bodhisattva *Saṁvara-śīla* comprises the sixty-four precepts observed by the Bodhisattva. These represent the natural pattern of behaviour of one who is devoted to the attainment of Enlightenment for the benefit of all. In other words, if you are devoted to the attainment of Enlightenment, or Buddhahood, not just for your own sake—not so that you can be 'up there' out of it all, looking down in pity on those still immersed in Samsara—but so that, having attained Enlightenment yourself, you can come back and help; and if this is your sole thought and aspiration, to which you subordinate everything else; then the way you act and speak—your natural pattern of behaviour—will coincide with the pattern reflected in the list of the sixty-four Bodhisattva Precepts. But once again it is not a question of having a list of rules and ticking yourself off against them one by one. It is a question of the living spirit, or heart, of the Bodhisattva, naturally expressing itself in a way that approximates to the Bodhisattva Precepts—or rather expressing itself in a way of which the precepts themselves are but an approximation.

Total action

Though the nature of Perfect Action should now be clear, there is one last matter to be considered. Perfect Action is also total action, or better, total act: that act in which the total man is involved. Most people are too divided, too fragmented, to act with the whole of themselves. Almost all the time we act with only a part of ourselves. When you go to the office or the factory, do you put yourself wholeheartedly into your work there? I think not. You might put quite a large slice of your energy into it, but quite a large slice remains at home, or is tied up elsewhere. You do not do your work with the whole of yourself; you do not give it your full attention, interest, and enthusiasm. If you have a hobby, you very rarely put the whole of yourself into the hobby, and you don't very often put the whole of yourself into your domestic life. There is something that is left out, or left over, so that we are all the time acting with only part of ourselves. Even when we are acting from what is best in ourselves, from our noblest impulses of kindness and generosity, that act is not a total act, inasmuch as there remain within us impulses of unkindness and ungenerosity from which, at the moment, we are *not* acting. Thus even our Right Action—even our so-called Perfect Action—remains imperfect in the sense that it is not total.

Perfect Action in the fullest sense is the prerogative of a Buddha: only an Enlightened mind can really act with the whole of itself, putting the whole of its wisdom and the whole of its compassion behind a particular act, with nothing left out or left over. This aspect of Buddhahood is represented by the Green 'archetypal' Buddha, Amogha-siddhi or 'Unobstructed Success'. Amoghasiddhi represents the total act at the highest conceivable level.

On rare occasions we may ourselves experience a foretaste of Perfect Action, in the sense of total action, on our own level of being. We may happen to be completely immersed in something. Every ounce of our energy, our effort, our awareness, our interest, our enthusiasm, our love, is involved at that moment. We are totally involved, both emotionally and intellectually. On such occasions we know that we are capable of putting the whole of ourselves into an act, without anything being left over. We know that we are capable, for an instant at least, of expressing ourselves fully and totally. The satisfaction and relief—the peace, even—which we then feel, we can get from no other source and in no other way. It is this state we should aim to be in all the time, at the highest level: the level of Buddhahood or Enlightenment. Then we shall really know what Perfect Action is, what total act is. Then we shall really understand, from the source, the principles of ethics.

V *The Ideal Society*
Perfect Livelihood

It will not be disputed that everybody dreams.
Psychologists tell us that we all dream four or five times a
night. We are even told that animals dream, as we can
sometimes see in the case of our pets. Not only does
everybody dream at night, when they are asleep, but
everybody day-dreams. On a warm, sunny afternoon
when, maybe, you are sitting on a park bench, and feeling
very comfortable and quiet, you just start day-dreaming.
This is something everybody does at some time or other.

The day-dream is, of course, usually a sort of wish
fulfilment, a Walter Mitty exercise. We dream of all the
things we would like to do and would like to be; and the
reason for this is that only too often we find everyday life
dull and uninteresting. We may have a tiresome, mono-
tonous job. We may be in circumstances which we dislike.
We may be having to associate with people with whom
we are not on particularly friendly terms. It may even be
that we find life not only dull and uninteresting, but
positively painful. We therefore try to get away from it and
create a world of our own outside ordinary existence. We
start day-dreaming in various ways. We start imagining a
better state of affairs. We start dreaming up some ideal
world, some ideal society, in which the imperfections of
this world and this society do not exist. Here there is
misery and unhappiness, but we like to day-dream about

some other place, some other world, where everybody is happy and where no doubt we can be happy too. Day-dreaming of this sort is not altogether a bad thing, provided we don't indulge in it too often, or when we really ought to be doing something else.

Though most day-dreaming is what may be described as unproductive fantasy, occasionally day-dreams are blueprints for the future. Today's dream may be, in some cases, tomorrow's reality. Looking at the history of the world, at the history of culture, of religions, of the arts, of philosophy, we find that the greatest men and women of the past have sometimes been the greatest day-dreamers. If we go back to the days of ancient Greece, to Plato—surely one of the greatest men who ever lived—we find that Plato too dreamed his dreams. The most famous of his dreams is *The Republic*, the great dialogue in twelve books in which Plato dreams his dream of an ideal society, the society based upon Justice. Moving to other times and cultures—and other dreams—we have in the *Book of Revelation*, the last book of the Bible, the marvellous vision of the new Jerusalem with its walls of jasper and gates of pearl—a vision of great archetypal and mythic significance. Coming nearer to our own times there is More's *Utopia*, Bacon's *New Atlantis*, Campanella's *City of the Sun*, and so on, down to H.G. Wells's *Men Like Gods*. These are all day-dreams of an ideal society, day-dreams of a world transfigured and transformed.

Buddhism too has its day-dreams. One Buddhist day-dream of the ideal society is found in the conception—or vision—of Sukhāvatī, the 'Pure Land' of Amitābha, the Buddha of Infinite Light, as described in some of the great Mahāyāna sutras. Especially as taught by the Shin schools of Japanese Buddhism, a Pure Land of the type represented by Sukhāvatī—the 'Happy Land'—is a place, a world, a plane of existence, where there is no pain, no suffering, no misery, no separation, no bereavement, no loss of any kind. It is a place where there is no old age, no sickness, and no death. It is a place of perfect peace in which there is no conflict, no war, no battle, nor even any misunderstanding—it is as perfect and happy as that! These great Mahāyāna sutras also tell us that the Pure Land or Happy Land is a place where there is no distinction of male and female, and where no one ever has to do any work. Food and clothing appear of their own accord whenever they are needed. In the Pure Land no one has anything to do except sit on their golden or purple or blue lotus at the feet of the Buddha and listen to his exposition of the Dharma. To crown it all, especially from our English point of view, we are told that in the Pure Land the weather is always perfect. This is a Buddhist day-dream, a vision of an ideal society and an ideal world.

This may all seem rather remote, rather archetypal and mythical, and not of much direct concern to us; but Buddhism, although it can dream, and dream very beautifully, is not content to leave it at that. The whole approach of the Buddha's teaching to these questions is very sane, very practical, and very realistic. Buddhism is not content to dream about some ideal society of the future, or some ideal world on another plane; it tries to create the ideal society, the ideal community, here and now on this earth. It tries, therefore, to transform, to transfigure, this society and this world into the image of the future, into the image of the Ideal; and it tries to do this in a number of different ways. One of these ways is the teaching of Right Livelihood, the fifth step of the Buddha's Noble Eightfold Path.

The preceding stages of the Noble Eightfold Path have been concerned with our initial spiritual experience of insight into the nature of existence, including ourselves, and the transformation by that experience of our emotional life, our communication with one another, and our ordinary everyday behaviour. In other words the Eightfold Path, so far, has been concerned with the transformation of our separate, individual selves. With this step, Perfect Livelihood, we are concerned with the transformation of the collective life, the life of the community, the life of society. This is an aspect of Buddhism which is not very much emphasized, in fact it is sometimes rather played down; but the idea that we should transform not only our individual lives but also society at large is very definitely a part of the total teaching.

Buddhism stands for the creation of an ideal society as well as for the creation of an ideal individual. After all we are all parts of society, all members one of another, and it is very difficult for us to change ourselves while society remains unchanged. The Indians have a proverb, 'You can't work in the kitchen without getting a bit of soot on you.' (Cooking in India is apt to be a rather messy affair.) In the same way you cannot live and work in a corrupt, basically unethical society without to some extent being besmirched by it. So even in the interests of one's own individual moral and spiritual life one has to make some effort to transform the society in which one lives. It is all very well to talk about the lotus blooming in the midst of the mire, but it is very difficult to be a lotus when the mire is particularly nasty and all-pervasive.

Our collective existence has three principal aspects— the strictly social aspect, the political aspect, and the economic aspect—and Buddhism has teachings which cover all three.

Buddhism has various social teachings, especially in the context of ancient Indian life. For example we find that the Buddha was not at all in favour of the caste system, which was a dominant feature of social life in India at his time, and still exists today. According to this system your position in society was dependent on your birth. If you were the son of a brahmin you were a brahmin, if you were the son of a trader you were a trader, and there was nothing you could do to change your status. Even now this system is very strong and all-pervasive in India, especially in the villages, and it has a stultifying effect upon human initiative generally. For this reason the Buddha said clearly and emphatically that the criterion which determines a person's position in society should not be birth, but worth. This is just one example of his social teaching.

In the same way we find that in the political sphere Buddhism upholds—or rather upheld in ancient times— the ideal of what is called Dharmarāja, a number of sutras being devoted to this topic. Dharma means truth, righteousness, reality. Rāja means king, or even government. Thus the ideal of the Dharmarāja represents the ideal of government by righteousness: the ideal that even in political affairs ethical and spiritual considerations and values should be paramount. It represents the idea that politics should not just be a cockpit of rival interests and factions, not just a question of manipulation and string-pulling, but that one should try to see the ethical and spiritual principles involved, and apply these to this aspect of one's collective existence.

In India the greatest example of this political ideal was the Emperor Aśoka. He was a great ruler of the Maurya dynasty, and lived about two hundred years after the Buddha. He inherited from his father the kingdom of Magadha, which he proceeded to expand, promptly swallowing up nearly all the other states of the sub-continent. A series of mopping-up operations increased the dimensions of Magadha even beyond those of present day India and Pakistan. The last state left for Aśoka to subdue, in the days before he became a Buddhist, was the state of Kalinga on the east coast, roughly corresponding to the modern state of Orissa. As Aśoka himself recorded in one of his

Rock Edicts, 'One-hundred-and-fifty-thousand persons were carried away captive, one hundred thousand were slain, and many times that number died.'

Seeing the havoc that had been wrought, Aśoka realized the misery brought about by war and by his own conquests. In his own words he 'felt profound sorrow and regret because the conquest of a people previously unconquered involved slaughter, death, and deportation ... even those who escaped calamity themselves are deeply afflicted by the misfortunes suffered by those friends, acquaintances, companions, and relatives for whom they feel an undiminished affection.' So he gave up this career of conquest—possibly the only example in history of a great conqueror who stopped in mid-career because he realized the moral wickedness of his actions. He stopped and he completely reversed. Instead of being known as Chandaśoka or Aśoka the Fierce, as he was before his 'conversion', he became known as Dharmaśoka or Aśoka the Righteous, and from that day onward seems to have considered himself the father of his people.

Aśoka did not give up his political path, but he quite explicitly proclaimed as his ideal the service of those he was supposed to be governing, and he upheld their welfare as the main object of his administration. He also gave great support to Buddhism, dispatching missionaries not only to different parts of India and Ceylon but also to Alexandria, Palestine, and Greece. Unfortunately so-called Buddhist rulers have not always followed in the footsteps of Aśoka. He is perhaps the only real example in Indian history of someone trying to apply Buddhist teaching directly to political life, and for that he deserves much credit. Some of you may be familiar with H.G. Wells's moving tribute to Aśoka in *The Outline of History*. 'Amidst the tens of thousands of names of monarchs that crowd the pages of history,' he writes, 'their majesties and graciousnesses and serenities and royal highnesses and the like, the name Aśoka shines, and shines almost alone, a star.'

The third aspect of our collective existence is the economic aspect. In this sphere Buddhism teaches Perfect Livelihood, that is to say it teaches the complete transformation, in the light of Perfect Vision, of the whole economic aspect of our collective life.

Now at this point a question arises. We have seen that our collective existence has three principal aspects, the social, the political, and the economic; but Perfect Livelihood represents only one of these, the economic. So why is this? Assuming that the fifth stage of the Noble Eightfold Path deals with our collective existence, why does it deal only with the economic aspect? Why are the political and social aspects not included in the Path? Why only Perfect Livelihood and not Perfect Citizenship or Perfect Administration? If the Path is concerned with our whole collective as well as our individual existence, why only Perfect Livelihood?

The answer to this question is partly to be found in the conditions obtaining in India in the Buddha's day. The social system was comparatively simple and unorganized —luckily—and apart from the caste system there was not much in this area which needed revision. In the political sphere, the Buddha taught and propagated the Dharma mainly in areas where monarchy was the only existing form of government, which means that ordinary people had little if any share in political life and activity. So in those days there was not much point in asking people in general to practise Perfect Government or Perfect Administration, or even Perfect Citizenship, when they had very little say in these matters. Everyone however had to work. They may not have had a vote or known what the king was up to, but they all had to earn a living, so the question of Perfect Livelihood was one which concerned everybody, even in the Buddha's day; and for this reason, no doubt, Perfect Livelihood was included in the Noble Eightfold Path. We might even hazard a speculation here and suggest that the Buddha himself felt that the economic aspect of our collective existence was more basic than either the social or the political aspect, and that for this reason too he included Perfect Livelihood, as representing that aspect, in the Noble Eightfold Path. During the Buddha's lifetime trade, business, and finance were all developing rapidly, and the Buddha could not have been unaware of this. A number of his closest lay disciples were what we would call merchant bankers, whose commercial interests extended as far as Babylon.

Having understood some of the main reasons for its inclusion in the Path, let us now try to investigate, in a little detail, what Perfect Livelihood really is. In so doing we should not forget that this stage of the Path stands for the transformation of our *whole* collective existence—our whole social life, our whole communal life—and not just for the economic aspect alone. In other words it stands for the creation of an ideal society: a society in which it is easier for us to follow the Path; a society in which, when we do follow the Path, we are not constantly having to go against everything that surrounds us, as tends to be the case at present.

As I have said, the Buddha included Perfect Livelihood in the Noble Eightfold Path because everybody had to work, and this of course still holds good. In fact one might say that this is now more than ever the case, because now —more than two-thousand-five-hundred years later—we spend more of our waking life working and earning a living than doing anything else. In the Buddha's day people at least had the rainy season off (during the rainy season it was not possible to work out of doors) but all we get now is two or three weeks at the seaside every year!

Since it occupies the greater part of our waking life, our livelihood will obviously have an important effect on our whole being. I do not think we always realize this. But if you do something for seven or eight hours a day, five days a week, fifty weeks a year, and if you do this for twenty, thirty, or forty years, it is not surprising if it leaves a mark on you, to say the least. The effect our working life has upon us is something we should consider and reflect upon. In the old days one could recognize the followers of certain trades by the physical effects. The dyer always had his hands deeply stained with dye from the vats, while the tailor would have a humped back. Even now one can often recognize an office worker by his rounded shoulders and general unathletic appearance.

These are just physical effects, but there is an even greater effect on the mind. The mind may be even more seriously deformed. The effects may not be easy to see, but they are there all the same, as in the case of the miraculous transformation of the picture of Dorian Gray. Every time he performed a wicked action his own face was not affected, but the face of the portrait was, until in the end the painting became a veritable picture of evil. Thus all the while our actions are producing an effect. Little by little a change is taking place. Your work, something you are engaged in every day, something you are up to your neck in for days, weeks, months, years, and decades, will have a tremendous—even a terrible—effect on the mind, very often without you knowing it. Just think what must be the mental state of a stockbroker, who is all the time preoccupied with stocks and shares, and who might have to pick up the telephone in the middle of the night because of a change in the market. Or think what must be the mental state of a bookmaker. That too must be pretty terrible.

Taking an even more extreme example, think what must be the mental state of a man who works in a slaughterhouse. We cannot close our eyes to the fact that there are hundreds if not thousands of slaughterhouses in this country, and hundreds of thousands of them all over the world. If we were to be asked here and now to take a knife and cut the throat of a cat, or to stamp on a rat or a mouse, most of us could not do it; but suppose you had to do it, twenty or thirty times a day. Suppose you had to cut the throat of a sheep, or to kill and skin a cow or a bull, twenty or thirty times a day, year after year. What would your mental state be *then*? And this is the occupation of tens of thousands, even hundreds of thousands, of people in the world today.

An Australian Buddhist monk I once knew told me that he had made a study of slaughterhouses in Australia, and the people who worked in them. He found a high incidence of serious mental disturbance—I think about sixty-six percent. Slaughterhouse workers usually lasted only two years. After that time human nature could stand it no more, and in most cases they reached a point where the mental disturbance was so serious they were unable to carry on. We should not think that this is something that does not concern us, because concern us it does. We are directly, morally involved, for it is our demand for meat that obliges people to earn their living and degrade themselves in this way.

With the help of these few—admittedly extreme—examples we can begin to see the importance of livelihood, and appreciate that without some measure of Right or Perfect Livelihood we can make very little spiritual progress. You can hardly imagine a slaughterhouse worker attending a weekly meditation class. It would not do them any good, even if they were able to sit still to meditate. I think I could guarantee that if such a person did come, and did try to meditate, before many weeks had passed they would be having horrible visions of the living beings they had slaughtered.

Buddhists in this country, I am glad to say, have begun to realize the importance of Perfect Livelihood. They have begun to realize that unless one conforms to this ideal, at least to some extent, little spiritual progress is possible. Among our English Buddhist friends there are, I know, people who have changed their jobs, sometimes at considerable financial sacrifice, for ethical reasons—because they felt that what they were doing was inconsistent with their profession of Buddhism, inconsistent with their Going for Refuge. This willingness on the part of some Buddhists to give up even a rewarding livelihood when it seems morally wrong is a very healthy development indeed. Until recently in this country, as in the West generally, interest in Buddhism was merely intellectual. People who might even have thought of themselves as Buddhists continued to live exactly as they did before they came across Buddhism, merely adding an interest in or study of Buddhism to their previous way of life. They made little if any attempt to change their lives in accordance with Buddhist principles, least of all in the economic sphere.

In the Buddhist scriptures the Buddha has a lot to say about Perfect Livelihood, usually explaining it in quite simple terms. First of all it is explained in terms of abstention from wrong livelihood—the negative coming before the positive. Various professions are strongly discouraged. At the top of the list comes earning a living by trafficking in living beings, whether humans or animals. This of course rules out the slave trade—two thousand and more years before Abraham Lincoln—and dealing in animals for the purpose of slaughter. It also rules out the profession of butcher or seller of meat. This is simple and obvious.

Also on the list is the purveying of poison. In the days of the Buddha there were people who dealt in poison, just as there were in Renaissance Italy. If you had an enemy and wanted to get rid of him quietly, all you had to do was pay a visit to a person of this kind, buy a small amount of poison, mix it with your enemy's food or drink, and that would settle the matter. We can think of all sorts of modern analogies, but there is no need for me to pursue these.

In the same way selling any kind of drink or drug that has a stupefying effect on the mind, or that diminishes one's awareness and sense of responsibility, is also a profession which is discouraged.

Perhaps of even greater interest is the Buddha's discouragement, if not actual prohibition, of any kind of dealing in weapons of war or armaments. If you are a follower of his teachings, he in effect declared, if you have gone for Refuge and consider yourself a Buddhist, you cannot possibly earn your living by manufacturing, selling, or in any other way dealing with weapons of war, which are instruments for taking the lives of other living beings. In the Buddha's day this was a very simple matter. It meant that you should not manufacture bows and arrows, swords or spears, or any other lethal weapon. But that was two-thousand-five-hundred years ago. Since then we have 'progressed' a great deal. We have become much more civilized, much more cultured, and we can kill much more easily and effectively, with atom bombs, hydrogen bombs, cobalt bombs, and so on. But the Buddha's principle of Perfect Livelihood still holds good.

If you have a few shares in a corporation which is helping to manufacture atomic or other such weapons, then you too are involved in helping to manufacture them, and to this extent you are, from the Buddhist point of view, involved in wrong livelihood. This point is too obvious to need much elaboration.

The Buddha also expresses his strong disapproval of various other trades which were carried on in the India of his day, and which are still carried on there today. These include earning money by palmistry and fortune-telling. Astrology and divination are also strongly discouraged. But such are the chances of history that in all the existing Buddhist countries many monks, I am sorry to say, do make money by divination, by telling fortunes, and by consulting the stars for their clients. Yet the Buddha clearly discouraged this, describing it as a wrong mode of livelihood.

It is interesting that the Buddha also disapproved of acting as a means of livelihood. Once an actor-manager called Talaputo approached him saying that there was a tradition among stage folk that when they died they went to the Heaven of the Laughing Gods, because by their acting they made people laugh, and wanting to know if the tradition was correct. At first the Buddha refused to answer Talaputo's question, but on being pressed he eventually did so. Far from going to the Heaven of the Laughing Gods, he told the actor-manager, actors went to hell when they died. The reason for this was that, themselves overcome by greed, hatred, and delusion, by their acting they increased the greed, hatred, and delusion of other people. Degraded themselves, they degraded others. For behaviour such as this the karmic recompense could not be other than painful.

It is very clear what sort of acting, what sort of stage performance, the Buddha was talking about. I personally do not believe his remarks would apply to classical Greek tragedy, for example, the effect of which is cathartic and which has, therefore, an ethical and spiritual significance. But certainly they would apply to the sort of performance Talaputo was in the habit of putting on, as well as to a great deal of the entertainment provided by modern stage and screen actors and actresses who, by their acting, often have an effect upon others which is degrading.

The principle that emerges from what has so far been said about Perfect Livelihood, in the sense of abstaining from wrong livelihood, is quite clear; but modern life is more complicated than life in the days of the Buddha, and I personally feel the whole subject of Perfect Livelihood needs reconsideration, if not restatement, in a more modern context. To do this it will be convenient to reconsider Perfect Livelihood under the headings of Occupation, Vocation, and Duration.

Occupation

Occupations or means of livelihood can be divided into four categories. Firstly there are those which, like working in a slaughterhouse, cannot be right under any circumstances. Secondly there are those which are not wrong in the obvious way that the first type are, but which definitely increase people's greed. Such occupations include working in the advertising industry, and producing luxury goods that people do not really need and have to be persuaded they want. Thirdly there are those occupations which *can* constitute Perfect Livelihood if one makes an effort. For example you might be a clerk working in the office of a firm that produces some quite good and necessary article, such as bread. If you work honestly and conscientiously at your job you can make it a form of Right Livelihood, even if not of Perfect Livelihood. Fourthly there are those occupations which do not involve undue mental strain. This is quite important nowadays, especially for those Buddhists who want to meditate. Even though your means of livelihood may not involve breaking any of the precepts, if it involves so much mental strain that you become tense and cannot meditate, then as a Buddhist you have to consider your position and try to find work of a less stressful nature.

Vocation
Vocation is the best form of livelihood, but it is very rare. We may define a vocation as a means of livelihood which is directly related to what one considers of ultimate importance in one's life. This will be different for different people. One thinks for example of medicine and the teaching profession. Someone might want to be a nurse out of a desire to relieve human suffering—which of course directly links up with Buddhism. Work in the arts or the various creative activities can also come into this category. If one pursues them in a creative spirit and does not commercialize them these also can be real vocations, and Perfect Livelihood in the best sense.

When one is practising Perfect Livelihood in the sense of following a true vocation there is no difference between one's work and one's play. You enjoy your work so much, and are so immersed in it, that you do not mind if you spend the whole of your waking life doing it. This is an ideal state, and one which people—often through no fault of their own—are rarely able to achieve.

Duration
We have already mentioned that people usually spend the greater part of their waking lives earning a living, just as they did in the time of the Buddha. But do they really need to? In my opinion they do not. Shocking as it may sound, in reply to the question, 'How much time should one devote to earning a living?' I would reply, 'As little as possible.' When I said this a couple of years ago at a meeting in London, an elderly friend of mine who happened to be present was deeply shocked. He remonstrated with me afterwards, saying, 'How could you say a thing like that publicly, in a lecture, with all those young people

there? You are simply encouraging them to be lazier and more useless than ever!' But in saying that one should devote as little time as possible to earning a living I am, of course, speaking especially to Buddhists, and—quite unrepentantly—to young people, since older people often have much less choice in the matter. Young people, I suggest, who have not yet launched into a career, and whose lives are still in the formative stage, should consider making just enough money to live on, very simply, and devoting the rest of their time to Buddhism—to the study of the Dharma, to meditation, and to helping to run the Buddhist movement.

They can do this in either of two ways. They can either have a regular part-time job which brings in enough money to live on, so that they are free to devote the rest of their time to Buddhism; or as some people do—though this is not so easy—they can work for a period of six months and then take six months off, supporting themselves on what they have been able to save out of their earnings and devoting *all* their time to Buddhism for a while. This does of course mean cutting down one's needs —or rather one's wants—but it is surprising how much one can cut down if one really makes up one's mind to do so.

Such a development would be good not only for oneself, it would also be good for Buddhism, because the Buddhist movement is expanding and we need more people. We need—and I hope I am not straying *too* far from tradition— people who will be part-time monks. In the Western Buddhist Order, now in process of formation, we hope to have a category of this sort—a category of people intermediate between on the one hand the ordinary lay person, fully immersed in the mire of Samsara and doing their best to bloom like a lotus in its midst, and on the other hand those who are committed in the full time way that the monk is.* Between these two extremes we need people who have one foot in the world and one foot in the spiritual dimension, to act as a bridge between the two. A category of people of this sort very definitely has a place in the modern world.

We have emphasized that Perfect Livelihood represents the transformation, in the light of Perfect Vision, of the society in which we live. Though Right or Perfect Livelihood pertains primarily to the economic aspect of our collective existence, we should not forget that the social and political aspects also have to be transformed. Perfect Livelihood, the fifth step of the Buddha's Noble Eightfold Path, represents the need to create an ideal society. After all we live in society and we cannot get away from it very much or for very long. We may go to a country retreat centre for a few weeks or months, if we are lucky, but eventually we have to come back and live in the world again, at least to some extent, even the luckiest of us. So we have to transform this world also, as part of the task of transforming ourselves.

We have mentioned the Western Buddhist Order, and this brings us to the topic of what in Buddhism we call the Sangha or Spiritual Community. There are a number of different ways of looking at the Sangha, but I am not going into them all now. In this connection I just want to sound one particular note, which seems particularly relevant here. The Sangha or Spiritual Community represents the ideal society on a very small scale. It is an anticipation, in miniature, of what society as a whole could be like further on in the course of human evolution. Our own small Sangha or spiritual community, our own small Order,

---

* This lecture was delivered in 1968, when the Western Buddhist Order was indeed 'in process of formation'. At the time of publication the WBO with its Indian wing the TBM consists of 416 members, many of whom are full-time Buddhists—some as members of Buddhist team-based 'Right Livelihood' businesses.

represents a society or a community fully based on ethical and spiritual principles. In other words it is not a society in the sense of an organization, but a real community based on these principles. This is how it differs from an organization. It also differs from an organization in respect of the degree of participation and commitment on the part of individual members.

It must also be stressed that what is of the utmost importance within the Sangha or Spiritual Community is right relationships between and among its various members. This cannot be stressed enough. If there is to be any real, genuine Buddhist movement in this country, as we hope there eventually will be, it can only grow out of a community of people who are ethically, psychologically, and spiritually in true contact and communication with one another—who are not just fellow members of an organization but friends, and related perhaps even more deeply than that on the spiritual plane. This is yet another aspect of the ideal society. We should feel that our own small Sangha, or Spiritual Community, our own small Order, is an exemplification on a small scale of the ideal society of the future—a society in which Perfect Livelihood is practised to the full, as unfortunately it is not practised in the world at large today.

VI *The Conscious Evolution of Man*
Perfect Effort

From Perfect Livelihood we pass to the sixth aspect of the Noble Eightfold Path, known in Sanskrit as *samyak-vyāyāma* (Pali *sammā-vāyāma*). Since the word *vyāyāma* is usually translated as 'effort', we shall speak of Perfect Effort here. We have seen that the second, third, and fourth stages of the Path deal with the transformation of the individual, while the fifth stage deals with the transformation of society as a whole. In the sixth stage, Perfect Effort, we are dealing again with the transformation of the individual, and specifically with the transformation of the individual will or volition; but Perfect Effort effects this transformation or transmutation against a very wide background indeed. The background of Perfect Livelihood is the whole community, society at large, but the background of Perfect Effort is nothing less than the whole range of sentient existence, the whole of life, the whole process of organic evolution. Within this context, and within the general framework of the Noble Eightfold Path, Perfect Effort represents the fact that the spiritual life is in a sense the continuation, the culmination, even the consummation, of the entire evolutionary process. For this reason Perfect Effort is sometimes spoken of in terms of the *conscious evolution of Man*.

As we have seen, the English word 'effort' is a translation of the Sanskrit *vyāyāma*, and in the modern languages of northern India such as Hindi, Gujerati, and Marathi, the latter is still current and still means physical exercise, especially in the sense of gymnastics. For instance when speakers of these languages want to translate the English —or rather Greek—word gymnasium they render it as '*vyāyāmaśālā*', or 'hall of exercise'. Thus we begin to get some idea of what the word connotes. This stage of *samyak-vyāyāma*, or Perfect Effort, draws our attention to a very important point: that the spiritual life is an *active* life. The spiritual life is not an armchair life. On the contrary it is active, even dynamic. Now this activity, this action, is not necessarily physical. That the spiritual life is an active life does not mean that you must be always rushing around 'doing things' in a crude, external, physical sense; but it certainly means that you should be mentally, spiritually, and even aesthetically active. In fact this stage of the Eightfold Path stands for the element of what we may call spiritual athleticism, which is a characteristic and prominent feature of Buddhism.

Generalizing, we may say that Buddhism is for the active. It is not for the mentally crippled or the spiritually bed-ridden. Buddhism is for people who are prepared to make an effort, who are prepared to try. Of course you may fail. You may fail ten times, twenty times, even a hundred times—but that doesn't matter so much. The important thing is that you should make the effort, that you should try. Buddhism is not for those who are only prepared to sit back comfortably in their armchairs and read all about the efforts of other people. You know the sort of thing: you take *The Life of Milarepa* and you ensconce yourself by the side of the fire with perhaps a cup of tea and a plate of muffins, and you sip your tea and munch your muffins, you are warm and cosy, and you read about the austerities of Milarepa and you think 'How fine!' and 'How wonderful!'

Buddhism is not like that. It is not just reading about other people's efforts, but being prepared to make at least a minimum of effort ourselves. For a long time a wrong image of Buddhism prevailed in Buddhist circles in this country. The impression was that Buddhism was intended primarily for old ladies—and when I say old ladies I am not being disrespectful to our female senior citizens, who are by no means necessarily old ladies in the sense in which I mean the term. I mean old ladies of both sexes and all ages. Far from being meant for people of this description Buddhism is a demanding and exacting Path, and as such is for the young and vigorous—either for those who are mentally and physically young, or at least those who are mentally and spiritually young, whatever the age and state of their bodies.

Perfect Effort is twofold. There is a *general* Perfect Effort, and a *specific* Perfect Effort. Though the sixth stage or limb of the Noble Eightfold Path is specifically concerned with Perfect Effort, some degree of effort is needed for all stages of the Path. We should not think that because one particular limb is labelled Perfect Effort you can undertake the other limbs without any effort at all. Some element of effort or striving is necessary for all parts of the Path, and this is what is meant by *general* Perfect Effort.

The Four Exertions
Specific Perfect Effort, which is Perfect Effort as represented by the sixth stage of the Path, consists of a set of exercises that are to be practised at this stage. These exercises are known as the Four Exertions. The Four Perfect Exertions—as they are also called—consist in (1) Preventing, (2) Eradicating, (3) Developing, and (4) Maintaining, and their common object is good and bad thoughts, or as we say in Buddhism, skilful and unskilful mental states. The effort which consists in *preventing* means the effort to

prevent the arising in our minds of those unskilful thoughts or mental states which have not yet arisen. Similarly, *eradicating* means eradicating from our minds those unskilful states which are already present therein. *Developing* means developing within our minds those skilful states which are not there already, while *maintaining* means maintaining within our minds those skilful states which already exist there. Thus Perfect Effort is primarily psychological. It consists in unremitting work on oneself and upon one's own mind by means of *preventing, eradicating, developing,* and *maintaining*.

This classification is given as an incentive and a reminder, because it is so easy to slacken off. People start with lots of enthusiasm: they are all for Buddhism, all for meditation, all for the spiritual life; but very often it quickly wears off. Enthusiasm wanes, and after a while it is almost as though it had never been at all. This is because the forces of inertia within ourselves, the forces holding us back and keeping us down, are very strong indeed—even in simple matters like getting up early in the morning to meditate. You might make a resolution to get up half an hour earlier, and you might succeed once or twice, or even three times; but by the fourth morning temptation will almost certainly have set in, and it will be a matter of quite serious mental struggle and conflict whether you get up or whether you stay a few minutes longer in that warm, cosy bed. You are nearly always the loser, of course, because the forces of inertia within ourselves are so strong. It is so easy for enthusiasm to wane, dwindle, and vanish.

Before we discuss these Four Exertions in detail there is one very important observation to be made. We cannot even begin to *prevent, eradicate, develop,* or *maintain* unless to begin with we know ourselves; that is to say unless we know which way our minds are going, or know what the contents of our minds are; and to know ourselves requires great honesty—at least, great honesty with ourselves. It is not expected that we should be completely honest with other people, but at least so far as the Four Exertions are concerned we should be honest with ourselves. (Those who find it surprising that complete honesty with other people is not to be expected of us should ask themselves if they realize how difficult this is. I remember reading that the first thing of which one became conscious on sitting down to write one's autobiography was all the things one was *not* going to tell, and this is very true. It is difficult enough for us to be honest with ourselves, not to speak of being honest with other people!)

If we want to practise the Four Exertions we must at least try to see ourselves as we truly are, so that we know what needs to be prevented, or eradicated, or developed, or maintained. Most of us have our own private dream-picture of ourselves. Closing our eyes we see ourselves as though in a mirror and think 'How beautiful! How noble!' This is the highly idealized picture which most of the time we have of ourselves. Not endowed, perhaps, with *all* the virtues, not *quite* perfect, but a really warm, lovable, sympathetic, intelligent, kind, well-intentioned, honest, industrious human being—*that* is what we usually see. What we have to try to develop, what we have to demand and almost to pray for is, in the words of the poet, the grace 'to see ourselves as others see us'; and to see ourselves as others see us is not easy. We have to undertake a mental stock-taking of our own skilful and unskilful mental states —our own 'vices' and 'virtues'. Though no moral absolutes are involved here, we at least have to understand our own minds, or our own mental states and mental qualities, very seriously and honestly before we can even think of applying the Four Exertions. Otherwise we shall not know how to proceed, and no real improvement—no real development—will be possible.

1. Preventing the arising of unarisen unskilful mental states

As we have seen, an unskilful mental state is one that is contaminated by craving or selfish desire, by hatred, or by delusion, mental confusion, bewilderment, and lack of perspective. A thought is said to be unskilful when it arises in association with one or more of these unskilful mental factors or mental states. Should it be asked where these unskilful thoughts come from—and we have to know where they come from if we want to eradicate them—the answer is that their immediate source (we are not concerned at the moment with their ultimate source) is the senses.

In Buddhism there are six senses: the five physical senses plus the mind, which is regarded as the sixth sense. This mind is the ordinary mind with which we carry on our lives. Unskilful mental states arise when, for example, you are walking along a street and, happening to notice something bright and colourful in a shop window, you at once think, 'I'd like to have that!' In this way through the organ of the eye there arises greed or craving. Sometimes we just remember something. As we sit quietly by ourselves a recollection of something we once had, or enjoyed, or thought, floats—we know not whence—into our mind, and before we realize what is happening we have been ensnared by craving, hatred, or fear.

Therefore in order to prevent the unarisen unskilful thoughts from entering the mind, and even taking possession of it and dominating it, it is necessary to have recourse to what is known in Buddhism as watchfulness or awareness with regard to the senses, especially the mind. This is traditionally known as 'guarding the doors of the senses'. Here the senses are pictured as being like the doors of a house. If you want to stop someone getting into the house you post a guard at the gate to examine the credentials of everyone who presents himself. Similarly you watch the doors of the six senses and try to see what impressions, what thoughts or ideas, are presenting themselves and seeking admission, and in this way the enemy is kept out. Watchfulness or awareness with regard to the workings of the physical senses and the lower mind must be kept up all the time. As we all know from experience, unskilful thoughts usually take us unawares: we do not even see them coming, do not see them entering the door. Before we know where we are they are right in the midst of our mind—sitting down in the house, as it were, very much at home—and we wonder how they got in! Well they got in through the door. They got in through one or another of the six senses. This is why we have to watch the doors of the senses if we want to keep out unskilful thoughts.

2. Eradicating arisen unskilful mental states
In terms of eradicating those unskilful mental states which are already present in the mind, we can discuss unskilful thoughts in terms of the Five Hindrances, a well known Buddhist teaching. The Five Hindrances are craving for material things, hatred, restlessness and anxiety, sloth and torpor, and doubt and indecision.

(a) The hindrance of craving for material things
Comprising as it does desire for such things as food, clothing, and shelter, the craving for material things is a very strong craving indeed. It is all right so long as we keep it within limits, but we do not usually do that. We usually want more material things than are really necessary, and in this way craving often gets completely out of hand. From being just the means of living and functioning in the world, material things become a definite hindrance to any kind of higher mental or spiritual life—even a hindrance to cultural life.

(b) The hindrance of hatred

This hindrance consists of hatred in all its gross and subtle forms: antagonism, aggressiveness, dislike, even righteous indignation. Only yesterday a woman came into our centre and tried to give us a little tract on the Messiah. We could not help getting into a conversation with her, and eventually the discussion turned to the Bible. She asked us what we thought about Jesus. We said that we certainly respected and even admired him, but there were a few things in the Gospels we could not quite understand. One of these was the way Jesus seemed to lose his temper with the money-changers in the temple, and drove them out. She said that this was righteous indignation, and did not come under the heading of anger. I said that Buddhists usually believe that a perfect man does not exhibit greed or anger or any such thing, but to this she replied that Christ was God, and with God it was different.

Unfortunately, as I pointed out to this woman, righteous indignation is the thin end of the wedge, and whether or not it was exhibited by Christ himself it opened the way, in Christian Europe, for all sorts of very unfortunate developments in the form of religious persecution, the Inquisition, the Crusades, and so on. Buddhism would say that all these unpleasant phenomena, which are sufficiently familiar to us from our study of history, are forms of violence, which is itself a manifestation of the hindrance of hatred. Instead of trying to rationalize the hindrances one should try to be honest with oneself and to see what one's mental state is really like.

(c) The hindrance of restlessness and anxiety

The hindrance of restlessness and anxiety is very much in evidence in modern Western society. You could hardly say that modern Western society was peaceful, or that it was calm and placid. You would have to say that it was restless, agitated, anxious, even tormented—and most of the people you meet are like this. They do not give an impression of peacefulness. With hardly any of them do you feel that you could sit down beside them and be at peace. Most people are consumed by worry, anxiety, restlessness, and haste. Sometimes it seems impossible just to sit quietly even for a few minutes. When one tries to meditate there is the noise of traffic, and of people rushing past. According to Buddhism, restlessness, worry, anxiety, haste of any kind is a hindrance. This does not mean that one should not sometimes do things quickly, but this is quite a different thing from a mental state of restlessness, when one turns restlessly from one thing to another because nothing really satisfies, and one does not know where to turn for something which will satisfy.

(d) The hindrance of sloth and torpor
The hindrance of sloth and torpor could also be described as inertia and stagnation—or becoming stiff and dry. People who get into this state feel that nothing matters. 'Why bother to make an effort? It's nothing to do with me. Just let things slide.' Nowadays this is a very common attitude. Frequently it is a reaction to restlessness and anxiety, but even so it is a hindrance. Often people try to rationalize it. Some people that you think are calm and quiet may simply be stagnating—just as others you think of as busy, active people may be merely restless.

(e) The hindrance of doubt and indecision
The hindrance of doubt and indecision is the inability—even the unwillingness—to think things out and come to a definite conclusion, a definite decision. It is the refusal to make up one's mind and then commit oneself—the refusal to take up a definite line of action, or to adopt a definite concrete attitude.

Such are the Five Hindrances, and when we speak of eradicating arisen unskilful mental states we are mainly referring to getting rid of the craving for material things, of hatred, sloth and torpor, restlessness and anxiety, and doubt and indecision.

In Buddhism the mind or consciousness is often compared to water. Water in its natural state is pure, translucent, and sparkling; but it can be contaminated in various ways. Similarly the mind, which is also pure by nature, can be defiled by the Five Hindrances. In Buddhist literature the mind that is full of craving is compared with water in which various colours—red, blue, green, yellow —have been mixed. There is a certain beauty, but the purity of the water—and of the mind—has been lost. The mind that is overcome by hatred is compared with water which, having reached boiling point, is hissing and bubbling and giving off steam. (Significantly, we speak of 'letting off steam' when we are angry.) In the same way, the mind that is disturbed by restlessness and anxiety is like water whipped into waves by a strong wind, while a mind that is in the grip of sloth and torpor is like a pond choked with weeds. As for the mind that is under the influence of doubt and indecision, it is like water which is full of evil smelling black mud.

But how is one to cleanse and purify the water? How is one to get rid of the Five Hindrances and eradicate all the arisen unskilful mental states? In Buddhism four methods are traditionally recommended, and they are usually tried in the order in which I shall now explain them.

The first method consists in considering the consequences of the unskilful mental state. If you allow yourself to get angry, what may happen? You may speak angrily, may speak harshly, and *that* may lead to unpleasantness or misunderstanding. If you get very angry, you may even strike someone. You may even kill someone. That is the logical result of anger if it is not checked and controlled. So reflect on the consequences of the unskilful mental state. This is the first method, and it can be applied to any of the hindrances. In the case of sloth and torpor for example you can reflect that if you go on stagnating you will not get anywhere or make any progress. In fact you will lose whatever you have already gained, whether materially or spiritually.

The second method consists in cultivating the opposite. Each unwholesome mental state has a positive wholesome counterpart. If you find on examination that your mind is overpowered by the unskilful mental state of hatred—if you dislike people, if you do not get on with them, do not think well of them—then cultivate the opposite of hatred, which is love, in the spiritual sense. Practise the *maitrī bhāvanā*, the development of loving kindness.* Hatred and love cannot exist in the mind simultaneously. If hatred is there, love cannot be there. If love is introduced, hatred has to depart.

The third method is to allow the unskilful thoughts simply to pass, without paying too much attention to them. One thinks, 'The mind is like the sky, and the unskilful thoughts are like the clouds. They come, and they go.' Do not get too upset about them or worked up over them. Do not beat your breast, or be unduly aware of them. Just let them go, let them pass, let them float away. Cultivate a 'witness-like' attitude towards them, just observing them in a detached manner, and reflecting that since they came into one's mind from outside and have nothing to do with one they are not, in fact, one's own thoughts. If you keep this up long enough, the unskilful

---

*As mentioned in Chapter 2, the *maitrī bhāvānā* (Pali *mettā bhāvanā*) is a meditation practice which encourages the development of strong feelings of well-wishing towards oneself and all other beings.

thoughts will usually go.

If these three methods do not succeed there is a fourth—forcible suppression. The Buddha says that if you cannot get rid of an unskilful mental state by any of the previous methods, then do it by force. Grit your teeth, and with an effort of will, suppress it. Notice that we say 'suppress' and not 'repress'. Repression is an unconscious process, but here you are acting quite consciously. You know what you are doing, and why; so that all the terrible consequences which the psychologists tell us come about as a result of repression will not occur when, as a last resort, you have recourse to this method.

But what if these four standard methods of eradicating the arisen unskilful mental thoughts fail? Sometimes it may happen that even when you grit your teeth and try to suppress it the unskilful thought simply will not go away. Like grass when the foot that was crushing it moves on, it springs up again as soon as the pressure is removed. When that happens, what can one do? Can one, in fact, *do* anything at all? If you are operating within a purely psychological context there is nothing whatever you can do; but if you are operating within a religious or spiritual—in this case a Buddhist—context, there is one final thing that you *can* do. We are told by the great masters of the spiritual life that if all these methods fail, and if however hard you try you cannot get rid of the hindrances, then the only thing left to do is to go for Refuge to the Buddha, together with your failure, and just let the matter rest there.

3. Developing unarisen skilful mental states
Developing those skilful mental states which have not yet arisen in our mind is not just 'thinking good thoughts' in the ordinary sense. It means the development of a higher state of consciousness and being: the transformation of the quality of one's whole personal existence. This transfor-

mation is possible with the help of meditation—not meditation by itself, but meditation as practised within the total context of the spiritual life. In Buddhism meditation is technically called '*bhavana*', which literally means 'making to become' or 'development'. The real aim of meditation is not just the concentration of the mind: that is just preliminary. The real aim of meditation is to transform consciousness—to make you a higher type of being than you were before you began practising it.

Progress in meditation—progress in the attainment of higher states of being—is marked or measured by the attainment of what we call the *dhyānas* (Pali *jhānas*). There are four of these *dhyānas*, or higher states of being and consciousness, each one more advanced than the one preceding it; and of course they are very difficult to describe. In Buddhist literature, especially in the Abhidharma, we have analyses of them, accounts of what mental factors are involved, but that does not really help us get the feel of them or know what they are like. It may be that a poetical description or an evocation of these higher states of consciousness will be of greater help to us, and fortunately for human weakness the Buddha himself does give a beautiful simile for each of the four *dhyānas*. In fact throughout Buddhist literature we find quite a number of beautiful and striking similes, many of which no doubt go back to the Buddha himself. I personally feel that this aspect of the Buddha's teaching method is insufficiently stressed. You must not think that the Buddha was dry and analytical. Often he presented his teaching in purely poetical and imaginative terms, and sometimes these convey the spirit of that teaching more successfully than the rather analytical descriptions on which some of his later followers tended to concentrate.

The simile for the first *dhyāna* or higher meditative state is that of soap powder mixed with water. A bath attendant, the Buddha said, takes a plateful of soap powder and mixes it with water. He kneads the two together until he has a ball of soap, every particle of which is saturated with water. At the same time there is not a drop of water in excess of what is required to saturate the ball. In this way in the first *dhyāna* the whole psychological being is saturated with the higher consciousness. Nothing overflows, and there is no particle of the being that is unpermeated. Those of you who have had any experience of this state, or any foretaste of it, will know what is meant. It is as though your ordinary being is suffused and penetrated by some higher element. 'You' are still there, but you are completely permeated by something of a higher nature.

As the simile for the second *dhyāna* the Buddha asks us to imagine a beautiful lake full to the brim with water. This lake is fed by an underground spring, so that fresh water is bubbling up within it all the time. Thus in the second *dhyāna* there bubbles up from the depths of the pure and translucent mind something even purer, something active and dynamic—as though you had tapped some inexhaustible source of inspiration.

Waxing even more poetical, as the simile for the third *dhyāna* the Buddha asks us to imagine a lotus growing in the water. This lotus is not only permeated by the water in which it grows, at the same time it is completely immersed in and surrounded by the water, so that there is water both within and without. Similarly in the third *dhyāna* you are not only permeated by the higher state of consciousness but contained within it, so that you live in it as in your natural element, and draw from it strength and nourishment.

The Buddha's simile for the fourth *dhyāna* is that of a man who wraps himself in a clean white sheet after taking a refreshing bath on a hot day, when he is tired and dusty. Just as the clean white sheet completely envelops the man, so in the fourth *dhyāna* the higher state of consciousness is all around, protecting and insulating you from the touch of the outside world. You are hermetically sealed within it, and though you are not out of communication with the outside world, so long as you remain in the fourth *dhyāna* no external thing can affect you.

Though with the attainment of the fourth *dhyāna* we have gone quite far, Buddhist tradition speaks of four states of consciousness which are in a sense higher still. These are the four 'formless spheres'. Though sometimes referred to as the four formless *dhyānas*, the four formless spheres are in fact subdivisions—or successive refinements—of the fourth *dhyāna*. Unlike the four *dhyānas* they are described in exclusively conceptual terms. First comes the 'sphere of infinite space', reflection on which has the effect of widening the mind and transporting it beyond its natural boundaries. Here one has the experience of absolute infinity, without limitation, or barrier, or obstacle. Beyond the 'sphere of infinite space' is the 'sphere of infinite consciousness', where one realizes that the mind itself is infinite. Far from being confined to the body it is conterminous with infinite space and therefore capable of expanding without limit in all directions. The third sphere is that of 'no-thingness' or 'non-particularity', which is not a state of blankness but an experience in which, though things are present, it is not really possible to distinguish one thing from another. To say that there is an underlying unity is a very crude way of putting it. Things lose their sharp edges, and no longer mutually exclude one another. The fourth sphere, the 'sphere of neither perception nor non-perception', is altogether beyond expression. There is no perception because of the extreme subtlety of the object, and no non-perception because the subject, though no less subtle, is nonetheless still there. The subject-object duality has been *practically* transcended.

Such are the four *dhyānas* and the four 'formless spheres', the successive attainment of which constitutes progress in meditation, or the development of unarisen skilful mental states.

In case anyone is wondering why we are dealing with meditation and the states of higher consciousness under the heading of Perfect Effort, rather than under that of Perfect Samadhi, the eighth stage of the Noble Eightfold Path, I should explain that meditation is of two kinds. There is that which depends upon conscious effort, and there is that which arises spontaneously as a natural result of our higher spiritual life. It is the first of these, meditation with effort, with which we are concerned, and which is meditation for all practical purposes. Indeed it is because meditation requires so much effort, and because it is, in fact, the major manifestation of effort within the context of the spiritual life and the Eightfold Path, that it is included here as part of Perfect Effort.

4. Maintaining arisen skilful mental states
Having prevented and eradicated negative mental states, and developed positive mental states, we now have to maintain the higher states of consciousness we have developed. It is very easy to slip back. If we stop our practice for even so much as a day or two we may well find ourselves back where we started months before. Regularity is therefore essential. If we give up after reaching a certain level and make no further effort, the result will be that we slip back even from that level. If however we continue to make an effort we shall eventually reach a stage from which it is impossible to regress. For most of us this stage is a long way ahead, and until we reach it we have to be constantly on our guard in order to maintain what we have developed.

The Background of Perfect Effort

Having examined Perfect Effort itself let us now look at the context or background against which it is practised. Just as the context of Perfect Livelihood is the entire community, in a similar way the background to our practice of Perfect Effort is the whole evolutionary process. Examining Perfect Effort against this background should make it clear that the spiritual life is a special phase of the evolutionary process, and that it constitutes what I have elsewhere called the Higher Evolution.

The concept of evolution is in many ways the dominant modern concept. Emerging in the sphere of biology, it was rapidly extended to all other departments of knowledge, so that nowadays we talk about the evolution of the solar system, the evolution of the arts, the evolution of religion, and so on. As Julian Huxley says, 'the different branches of science combine to demonstrate that the universe in its entirety must be regarded as one gigantic process, a process of becoming, of attaining new levels of existence and organization, which can properly be called a genesis or an *evolution*.' Since man is part of the universe, part of nature, man too is in process of becoming, man too is constantly attaining new levels—not just new forms—of existence and organization. Far from being created at a stroke, as people used to think, man has *evolved*—and is evolving still.

Now any evolving phenomenon can be studied in two ways: in terms of the past or in terms of the future, genetically or teleologically. Suppose then that we take the phenomenon of man at the best we usually know him—as a self-conscious, aware human being, who is intelligent, sensitive, and responsible. We can try to understand man in terms of what he has developed out of, and also in terms of what he will—or at least could—develop into. The first—what we have developed out of—constitutes the

Lower Evolution. This is the subject matter of science, especially of biology and anthropology. The second— what we will or can develop into—constitutes the Higher Evolution. This is the province of the higher or universal religions, and especially of Buddhism.

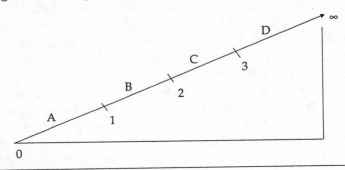

0 Starting point of evolutionary process.
1 Rudimentary human consciousness emerges.
2 Emergence of self-consciousness.
3 Beginnings of transcendental awareness—Stream-entry.
∞ Nirvana, Enlightenment, or Buddhahood.
A Infra-human stage of evolution.
B Human stage, primitive and civilized.
C Ultra-human stage, arts and sciences, culture, and lower religions.
D Trans-human

The relationship between the Lower and Higher Evolution is best explained with the help of a diagram. This consists of a line, or rather an arrow, along which are various symbols, figures, and letters. The point marked 2 in the centre of the line represents the self-conscious, aware human being. From the bottom of the line, marked 0, up to point 2, represents the Lower Evolution. From point 2 upwards represents the Higher Evolution. Each of these two sections, from 0 to 2 and from 2 upwards to infinity, can in turn be divided. Point 1, intermediate between 0 and 2, is the point at which rudimentary human consciousness emerges. This is the point at which the

128

animal becomes, or at least begins to become, man—an event that happened not so very long ago. (The relative distance between the points bears, of course, no relation to the actual length of time involved.) Point 3, between point 2 and infinity, represents the point at which Transcendental awareness begins to emerge. This is the point of Stream-entry, or of non-regression or irre-versibility—or even of Perfect Vision, at least in its rudimentary form.

Moving upwards along our line, 0 represents the starting point of the whole evolutionary process. In terms of physics this could be the so-called Big Bang; for biology it could be the emergence of the simplest forms of life. Point 1 represents the stage at which human consciousness emerges. Point 2 is the stage at which self-consciousness or awareness emerges—most of us are still a little below this point, though some are a little above it. Point 3 represents the stage at which Transcendental awareness, in the sense of awareness of Reality, emerges. This is the stage of conversion in the true sense. It is the Point of No Return. The symbol for infinity towards which our arrow points represents Nirvana, Enlightenment, or Buddhahood.

Points 1, 2, and 3 divide our arrow into four sections, marked not by numbers but by letters. Section A represents what may be described as the infra-human stage of evolution, and comprises the mineral and vegetable king-doms, and the animal kingdom exclusive of man. Section B represents the human stage, both primitive and civi-lized. Stage C represents what we may call the ultra-human stage of evolution. It is at this stage that the arts and sciences, culture, and the lower religions are found. Finally, section D represents the supra-human or trans-human stage. Thus our arrow covers the entire process of evolution, from the simplest forms of life through to man —unenlightened man—and onwards to the Buddha or

Enlightened man. Science and religion, the Lower and the Higher Evolution, are embraced in one enormous sweep, and this is a most inspiring and invigorating prospect. Closing one's eyes one can see the whole process of growth and efflorescence, as from its first beginnings it passes through innumerable successive steps and stages. One can see the long, slow, painful ascent of life as it culminates—*for the present at least*—in man.

Perfect effort as conscious evolution

Perfect Effort is of course the sixth stage of the Noble Eightfold Path, and the Noble Eightfold Path corresponds, strictly speaking, to the fourth stage of the evolutionary process—to the stage represented by section D of our line. In a wider sense, as comprising what we might call the mundane as well as the Transcendental Eightfold Path, it corresponds to the whole process of the Higher Evolution, that is to the stage represented by sections C and D of the line. As such it includes in its scope even our relatively half-hearted attempts to follow the Eightfold Path.

As our diagram suggests, the Lower and the Higher Evolution are in one sense continuous; but in another sense they are not. There are in fact important differences between them. Whereas the Lower Evolution is collective, for here it is the whole species that evolves, not any one individual—at this level the individual does not yet exist —the Higher Evolution is an individual affair. One individual can evolve ahead of another and outstrip the whole of the rest of the human race. This possibility presupposes self-consciousness or awareness, and it is for this reason that we speak of the *conscious* evolution of man. It also presupposes individual *effort*—which is why Perfect Effort features so prominently in the Buddha's Noble Eightfold Path, whether as corresponding to section D alone, or to both sections C and D of our diagram.

We have evolved to our present human level collectively. For the most part we have come up together, but further progress requires a further effort on the part of each individual. In other words further progress requires Perfect Effort, both general and specific. It requires that we have recourse to the Four Exertions: to *preventing* and *eradicating* in respect of bad thoughts, and *developing* and *maintaining,* in respect of good thoughts. Ever practising Perfect Effort in this way, we shall reach the end of the Path, which means that we shall attain Nirvana, Buddhahood, or Reality.

VII *Levels of Awareness*
Perfect Awareness

We have seen that the Higher Evolution is distinguished from the Lower by the fact that it takes place in and through awareness. It follows, therefore, that progress in the Higher Evolution is at the same time a progress in awareness. Since this progress is measured by the achievement of successively higher states, this introduces the idea of levels of awareness. It is these levels of awareness which are the subject matter of the seventh stage of the Noble Eightfold Path, usually called Right Mindfulness; it is these levels we must investigate if we want to know what the term 'Right Mindfulness', or 'Perfect Awareness', really conveys.

In Sanskrit this stage is called *samyak-smṛti* (Pali *sammā-sati*). *Smṛti*, or *sati*, is usually translated as 'mindfulness', or sometimes as 'awareness', but the literal meaning of both words is simply memory or recollection. The word has several shades of meaning, and these are not always easy to disentangle. I am therefore going to approach the question of the meaning of the word *smṛti* or mindfulness rather indirectly, by taking an example from everyday life. This will be—to begin with—an example not of mindfulness but of unmindfulness, because we are more familiar with unmindfulness than with mindfulness, and by analysing unmindfulness we shall perhaps be more easily able to arrive at some conception of mindfulness.

Suppose, then, that you are writing a letter, an urgent letter that it is imperative should go off by the next post. But as so often happens in modern life the telephone rings, and it is some friend of yours wanting a little chat. Before you know where you are you are involved in quite a lengthy conversation. You go on chatting maybe for half an hour, and eventually, the conversation completed, you put down the phone. You have talked about so many things with your friend that you have quite forgotten about the letter, and you have talked for such a long while that you suddenly feel quite thirsty. So you wander into the kitchen and put the kettle on for a cup of tea. Waiting for the kettle to boil you hear a pleasant sound coming through the wall from next door, and realizing it is the radio you think you might as well listen to it. You therefore nip into the next room, switch on the radio, and start listening to the tune. After that tune is finished there comes another, and you listen to that too. In this way more time passes, and of course you've forgotten all about your boiling kettle. Whilst you are in the midst of this daze, or trance-like state, there is a knock at the door. A friend has called to see you. Since you are glad to see him you make him welcome. The two of you sit down together for a chat, and in due course you offer him a cup of tea. You go into the kitchen and find it full of steam. *Then* you remember that you had put the kettle on some time ago, and *that* makes you remember your letter. But now it is too late. You have missed the post.

This is an example of unmindfulness in everyday life. Indeed everyday life consists, for the most part, of this sort of unmindfulness. We can all no doubt recognize ourselves in the portrait. We can recognize that this is the chaotic, unmindful fashion in which, for the most part, we live our lives.

Now let us analyse the situation, to give ourselves a

better understanding of the nature of unmindfulness. First of all in our example we see the plain and simple fact of forgetfulness, which is a very important element in unmindfulness. We forget about the letter which we are writing when we are talking on the phone, and we forget the kettle which is boiling for tea when we are listening to the radio.

Why do we forget so easily in this fashion? Why is it we lose sight of something we ought to be bearing in mind? The reason is that we are very easily distracted. Our mind is very easily turned away or turned aside. It often happens for instance that I am giving a lecture or talk of some kind. Everybody is paying close attention, and there is a pin-drop silence. But then the door opens, and someone comes in. And what happens? Half the heads swivel round as though they had all been pulled by the same string. People are as easily distracted as that. Sometimes it is a bluebottle buzzing against the window-pane, or the dropping of a sheet of my notes that distracts people. Such things show how easily we are distracted, which is why we tend to forget in the affairs of everyday life.

Why is it that we are so easily distracted? How does it come about? We are easily distracted because our concentration is weak. If for instance you were really listening to me, and really concentrating on what I was saying, an elephant could come in at the door and you would not notice it. Because we are *not* concentrated in this way distraction occurs very easily. We do not concentrate wholeheartedly on what we are doing. Usually we attend to what we are doing or saying or thinking only in a half-hearted way.

Why is our concentration so weak? Why are we so half-hearted? Our concentration is weak because we have no continuity of purpose. There is no one overriding purpose that remains unchanged in the midst of all the different things that we do. We switch from one thing to another, one wish to another, all the time, like the character in Dryden's famous satire who

> Was everything by starts, and nothing long;
> But in the course of one revolving moon
> Was chymist, fiddler, statesman, and buffoon.

Because there is no continuity of purpose, because we are not bent on one main thing all the time, we have no real individuality. We are a succession of different people, all of them rather abortive or embryonic. There is no regular growth, no real development, no true evolution.

Some of the main characteristics of unmindfulness should now be clear. Unmindfulness is a state of forgetfulness, of distraction, of poor concentration, of an absence of continuity of purpose, of drift, and of no real individuality. Mindfulness of course has just the opposite characteristics: it is a state of recollection, of undistractedness, of concentration, of continuity and steadfastness of purpose, and of continually developing individuality. All these characteristics are connoted by the term 'awareness', and especially by Perfect Awareness. This is not to say that Perfect Awareness is fully defined by these characteristics, but they will serve to give us a general idea of what mindfulness or awareness is, and of what Perfect Awareness is.

Levels of awareness

Now let us turn to the main theme of our discussion of Perfect Awareness, which is levels of awareness. Traditionally these levels are arranged or ordered in various ways, but here I propose to discuss them under four principal headings: awareness of things, awareness of self, awareness of other people, and lastly awareness of Reality, of Truth, of the Ultimate. By considering the levels of awareness under these four main headings we shall, I hope, be able to obtain a fairly comprehensive idea of the true nature of Perfect Awareness.

1. Awareness of things

When we speak of awareness of 'things' we mean material things such as a book or a table. We mean our whole material environment, full of so many different objects. We mean, in short, the whole realm of nature. Most of the time we are only vaguely conscious of the things around us, and have no more than a peripheral awareness of them. We are not really aware of our environment, not really aware of nature, not really aware of the cosmos, and the reason for this is that we seldom or never really stop and look at them. How many minutes of the day—not to speak of hours—do we spend just looking at something? Probably we do not even spend seconds in this way, and the reason we usually give is that we have no time. This is perhaps one of the greatest indictments of modern civilization that could possibly be made—that we have no time to stop and look at anything. We may pass a tree on the way to work, but we have no time to look at it, or even to look at less romantic things such as walls, houses, and fences. This makes one wonder what this life, and this modern civilization of ours, is worth if there is no time to look at things. In the words of the poet:

> What is this life, if full of care
> We have no time to stand and stare?

Of course the poet has used the word 'stare' for the sake of the rhyme, and what he really means is not staring in the literal sense but just looking and seeing. The fact that we have no time for this is something of which we need to remind ourselves. Yet even if we do have time to stop and look and try to be aware we hardly ever see things in themselves. What we usually see is our own projected subjectivity. We look at something, but we see it through the veil, the curtain, the mist, the fog of our own mental conditioning.

Some years ago in Kalimpong I went for a walk with a Nepalese friend, and we happened to stop at the foot of a magnificent pine tree. As I looked up at the smooth trunk and the mass of deep green foliage I could not help exclaiming, 'Well, isn't that a beautiful tree!' My Nepalese friend, who was standing beside me, said, 'Oh yes, it is a beautiful tree. There's enough firewood there for the whole winter.' He did not see the tree at all. All he saw was a certain quantity of firewood. Most of us look at the world of material things in just this way, and it is an attitude from which we have to free ourselves. We have to learn to look at things themselves, for their own sake, untainted by any trace of subjectivity, personal preference, or desire.

This attitude or approach is much emphasized in Far Eastern Buddhist art, that is in the art of China and Japan. In this connection there is the story of a certain apprentice painter who once asked his master, a celebrated artist, how to paint bamboos. The master did not however say that you take your brush and make certain strokes on the silk or the paper. He did not say anything about brushes or pigments, or even about painting. He only said, 'If you want to learn to paint bamboos, first learn to *see* bamboos.' This is a sobering thought—that we rush to paint something when we have not even looked at it—but this is what many artists actually do, or at least what many amateurs in art do. So the disciple, we are told, just looked. He went about *looking at bamboos*. He looked at the stems, and he looked at the leaves. He looked at them in the mist, and in the rain, and in the moonlight. He looked at them in spring, in autumn, and in winter. He looked at large bamboos, and he looked at small bamboos. He looked at them when they were green, and when they were yellow, when they were fresh and springy, and when they were dry and decayed. In this way he spent several years, just looking at bamboos. He became genuinely aware of the bamboos. He really *saw* them. And seeing them, being aware of them in this way, he became at one with the bamboos. His life passed into the life of the bamboos. The life of the bamboos passed into his life. Only then did he paint bamboos; and of course you may be sure that it was real bamboos that he painted. In fact we might say that it became a question of a bamboo painting bamboos.

According to Buddhism, at least according to Far Eastern Buddhism—the traditions of China and Japan and, above all perhaps, the traditions of Ch'an and Zen—this should be our attitude towards all material things. This should be our attitude towards the whole of nature: not only towards bamboos, but towards the sun, the moon, the stars, and the earth; towards trees and flowers and human beings. We should learn to look, learn to see, learn to be aware, and in this way become supremely receptive. Because of our receptivity we shall become one with, or at least fused with, all things; and out of this oneness, this realization of affinity and deep unity, if we are of artistic temperament we shall create, and truly create.

2. *Awareness of oneself*
Awareness of oneself has many different sub-levels, of which three are of particular importance. These are awareness of the body, awareness of feelings, and awareness of thought.

(a) *Awareness of the body and its movements.*
In the sutras the Buddha encourages his disciples to be constantly aware of the body and its movements. One should be aware when one is walking, sitting, standing, or lying down. One should be aware of the position of the

hands and of the feet, of how one is moving, how one is gesturing, and so on. According to this teaching one cannot, if one is aware, do anything is a hasty, confused, or chaotic fashion. We have a wonderful example of this in what is known as the Japanese tea ceremony. On the face of it the Japanese tea ceremony revolves around a very ordinary act, which we do every day: the making and drinking of a cup of tea. This is something we have all done hundreds and thousands of times. But how do they do it in Japan? How is it done in the Japanese tea ceremony? There it is done in a quite different way, because it is done with awareness.

With awareness the kettle is filled with water. With awareness it is put on the charcoal fire. With awareness one sits and waits for the kettle to boil, listening to the humming and bubbling of the water and watching the flickering of the flames. Finally with awareness one pours the boiling water into the teapot, with awareness one pours out the tea, offers it, and drinks it, all the time observing complete silence. The whole act is an exercise in awareness. It represents the application of awareness to the affairs of everyday life. This attitude should be brought into all our activities. All should be conducted on the same principle as the Japanese tea ceremony, everything being done with mindfulness and awareness, and therefore with stillness, quietness, and beauty, as well as with dignity, harmony, and peace.

But if the Japanese tea ceremony represents a certain level of awareness in everyday life, and a certain type of spiritual culture—that of Far Eastern Buddhism, especially Zen—what analogous ceremony or institution is there which represents the attitude of the West today? What do we have that breathes the whole spirit of our commercial culture? After turning this question over in my mind, I decided that what was characteristic of our culture was the business lunch. In the business lunch you are trying to do two things at the same time: trying to have a good meal, and trying to pull off a good deal. This sort of behaviour, where one is trying to do two contradictory things at once, is quite incompatible with any true, real, or deep awareness. It is also very bad for the digestion.

Awareness of the body and its movements will, if practised continually, have the effect of slowing these movements down. The pace of life will become more even and more rhythmical. Everything will be done more slowly and deliberately. But that does not mean that we will do less work. That is a fallacy. The person who does everything slowly because he does it with awareness and deliberation may well accomplish more than the person who looks very busy because he is always dashing around and has lots of papers and files on his desk, but who is in fact not busy but just confused. A really busy person goes about things quietly and methodically, and because he doesn't waste time in trivialities and fuss, and because he is aware, in the long run he actually gets more done.

(b) Awareness of feelings

In the first place awareness of feelings means being aware of whether we are happy, whether we are sad, or whether we are in a dull, grey, neutral state somewhere in between. By becoming more aware of our emotional life we will find that unskilful emotional states—those connected with craving, hatred, or fear—will tend to be resolved; whereas the skilful emotional states—those connected with love, peace, compassion, and joy—will tend to be refined. For instance, if we are by nature a bit hot-tempered and prone to anger, then as we develop awareness of feelings we shall first of all be aware of our angry feelings when we have *been* angry. With a bit of practice we shall be aware that we are *being* angry. And with more practice we shall be aware that anger is on the point of *arising*. If we continue to apply awareness to our emotional life in this way, unskilful emotional states like anger will eventually subside, or at least be brought under control.

(c) Awareness of thought
If they are suddenly asked 'What are you thinking of just now?' most people have to confess that they do not know. This is because often we do not really think, we just allow thoughts to drift through the mind. We are not clearly aware of them, we are only vaguely conscious of our thoughts in a grey, twilight sort of way. There is no directed thinking. We do not decide to think about something and then actually think about it. Ideas drift through our mind in a vague, loose, and woolly manner. They drift in and they drift out, sometimes just eddying, curling, and winding round and round inside the mind.

We therefore have to learn to watch from moment to moment to see where the thoughts come from and where they go. If we do this we shall find that the flow of thoughts will be reduced, and that the mental chatter which goes on all the time will be stopped. Eventually, if we persist in this awareness of thought for long enough, the mind will become, at certain points—certain peaks in meditation practice—completely silent. All discursive thoughts, all ideas and concepts, will be wiped out, and the mind will be left silent and empty, but at the same time full. This silence or emptiness of the mind is much more difficult to achieve, or to experience, than any mere silence of the tongue; but it is at this point, when as a result of awareness the mind becomes silent and thoughts vanish, leaving only the pure, clear awareness or consciousness behind, that real meditation begins.

These three kinds of awareness of oneself—awareness of the body and its movements, awareness of feelings and emotions, and awareness of thoughts—should be practised, we are told, all the time, whatever we are doing. All through the day and even, with practice, at night— even in the midst of dreams—we should continue to be aware. If we are aware in this way all the time: aware of how our body is disposed, how we put down our foot or raise our arm; aware of what we are saying; aware of our feelings, whether happy, sad, or neutral; and aware of what we are thinking, and whether that thinking is directed or undirected—if we are aware in this way all the time, even for the whole of our lives if possible, then we shall find that gradually and imperceptibly, but none the less surely, this awareness will transmute and transform our whole being, our whole character. Psychologically speaking, awareness is the most powerful transforming agent that we know. If we apply heat to water then the water is transformed into steam. In the same way, if we apply awareness to any psychic content, the content is refined and sublimated.

3. *Awareness of people*

If we are aware of people at all we are usually aware of them not as human beings but as things or objects 'out there'. In other words, we are aware of them as physical bodies impinging on our physical bodies. This way of being aware of other people is not enough. We must become aware of them as persons.

How is this done? How is one to become aware of another person as a person? In the first place of course one must look at them. This sounds simple, but it is in fact very difficult. When I say 'look at them' I do not mean stare. We should not fix them with a hypnotic gaze. We should just look—and this is not so easy as it sounds. It would not be exaggerating too much to say that some people have never really looked at another person, while some have never really been looked at. It is indeed possible to go through one's whole life without either looking at another person or being looked at in one's turn; and if we do not look at other people we cannot be aware of them.

As part of our FWBO activities we sometimes do what are called communication exercises. There are four of these exercises, the first of which consists in 'just looking', that is, in sitting and simply looking—without tension or embarrassment, and without bursting into hysterical laughter—at the person seated opposite, who is looking back. This exercise comes first because there cannot be any real communication with another person, or any real exchange, unless you are aware of that person. Communication is of course a whole subject in itself. I touched on it in connection with Perfect Speech, and all that I need repeat here is that communication is by no means confined to speech. It can also be so direct and subtle as to be virtually telepathic. When communication is of this type it usually indicates rather a high level of awareness in people. Moreover such 'telepathic' awareness is usually mutual.

In India there is an important form of awareness of others which is known as *darśan*. This means literally a sight or a seeing—a vision—and it is the term used for awareness of the spiritual teacher. In India spiritual teachers usually have what are called ashrams, which are sort of retreat centres where the teacher lives, where his disciples gather round him, and where people come to see him. In such ashrams the usual form is that after an evening service called *āratī*, which involves the waving of lights in front of the image of whatever Hindu deity is worshipped, the teacher just sits there and people come. In the case of famous teachers people come from all over India. They come not just in hundreds but in their tens of thousands, and all they do is sit and look at the teacher. They 'take his *darśan*'. In other words they do their best to be aware of him—aware of him as a spiritual person, or as the living embodiment of a spiritual ideal.

In the case of the celebrated Ramana Maharshi, whom I mentioned while discussing Perfect Speech, he used to sit in his ashram 'giving *darśan*' for weeks and months on end. I believe he sat for about fifty years on one particular spot and, as I saw myself, people used to come from all over India to see, to look, to be aware of him. Very often they did not ask any questions, or enter into discussion. Some of course did, but the majority just sat, looked, and were aware. They 'took *darśan*'. According to Indian spiritual tradition it is not enough to learn by listening to the teacher's instruction. One must also be aware of him as a spiritual person. Without this kind of awareness very little will be gained from the teacher. One may gain intellectually, but one will not gain spiritually.

4. Awareness of Reality

Awareness of Reality does not mean thinking about Reality; it does not even mean thinking about being aware of Reality. The best way we can describe it is to say that awareness of Reality is a direct, non-discursive contemplation. It has of course many forms, only one or two of which I am going to mention.

One of the best known and most widely practised of these forms is known as the recollection—or awareness—of the Buddha, the Enlightened One. By this is meant awareness of the person of the Buddha, in the sense of awareness of Reality as embodied in the form of the Enlightened human teacher. When practising this as a regular exercise one usually begins by being inwardly aware of the external appearance of the Buddha—of what he might have looked like as he trod the roads of India two-thousand-five-hundred years ago. One sees, or one tries to see, the tall serene figure in the yellow robe as he walked from one end of northern India to another, preaching and teaching. Then one sees—tries to be inwardly aware of—the Buddha at certain important moments in his career, especially when he sat beneath the Bodhi tree, repulsed the armies of Māra within his own mind, and gained Enlightenment. Various other episodes can also be imagined.

Then one recollects, becomes aware of, the attributes or spiritual qualities of the Buddha: the boundless wisdom, the infinite compassion, the great peace, the immaculate purity, and so on. From being aware of those attributes one tries to pierce through to their common innermost essence. One tries to pierce through to the Buddhahood of Buddhahood, the Enlightenment of Enlightenment, and to become aware of *that*. In other words one tries to become aware of Reality itself expressing itself through—even shining through—the person or the figure of the Buddha, the Enlightened One.

One can also practise, along the same lines, the awareness of *Śūnyatā* or voidness: awareness of Reality as empty of all conceptual content, and beyond the reach of thought and imagination, and even of aspiration and desire; but this sort of awareness of Reality in its nakedness can be practised only after some previous experience of meditation.

Awareness of Reality is the most difficult of all the levels of awareness to maintain. Because of this various methods have been developed to help us maintain constant recollection or awareness of Reality, of the Ultimate, the Transcendent. One of these is the constant repetition of a *mantra*, a sacred word or syllable, or string of syllables, which is connected, usually, with a particular Buddha or Bodhisattva. The repetition of this *mantra* over and over again—of course after one has been properly initiated—not only puts one in contact with that which it represents, but keeps one in contact with it in the midst of all the vicissitudes, all the ups and downs, even all the heartbreaks and tragedies, of daily life. Eventually this repetition becomes spontaneous (*not* automatic), welling up all the time, even independently of one's personal volition, so that a slender thread of contact with Reality is maintained even in the midst of all the avocations and duties, the responsibilities and trials, and pleasures too, of ordinary human existence.

Such are the four principal levels of awareness: awareness of things, awareness of oneself, awareness of people, and, above all, awareness of Reality. Each one of these has its own distinctive effect on the person practising it. Through awareness of things, as they really are, we become free from the taint of subjectivity. Awareness of oneself refines our psychophysical energy. Awareness of people stimulates. Finally, awareness of Reality transmutes, transfigures, and transforms.

All these different kinds of awareness contribute, in their own distinctive way, to the process of the Higher Evolution. They one and all between them bring one very near to the last stage of the Path—Perfect Samadhi.

VIII   *The Higher Consciousness*
Perfect Samadhi

We have been following, in imagination at least, the Buddha's Noble Eightfold Path, and with the eighth and last stage of that path we come to the end of our long journey. This last stage is *samyak-samādhi* (Pali *sammā-samādhi*), usually translated—not very adequately—as Right Meditation. I do not propose to offer any simple translation for the Sanskrit word *samādhi*; instead I will refer to this last stage of the path simply as Perfect Samadhi. What this *really* means will, I hope, become clear as we proceed.

As a general rule the more advanced the stage of spiritual development, the less there is to say about it. This principle holds good throughout the whole of the spiritual life. In the Pali scriptures, for instance, we find that whereas the Buddha had a lot to say about ethics, and went into questions of personal behaviour in considerable detail, when it came to Nirvana, the ultimate goal, he said very little. Indeed there was little for him to say! Thus although the Buddhist Scriptures are very extensive and deal with a vast number of topics, on the whole they do not tell us much about Nirvana. The Buddha was not very communicative on this particular subject. Indeed when questioned about Nirvana, or about the nature of Enlightenment, or the experience of the Enlightened person, he sometimes remained perfectly silent. In worldly life of course the more we have to say about something the more important we consider it to be. If an issue is being discussed at great length in the media everyone assumes it must be very important. But in the spiritual life the less one has to say about something, or the less one is able to say, the more truly important it is.

This principle holds good with regard to the Noble Eightfold Path. One can say a lot about Perfect Speech, Perfect Action, and Perfect Livelihood; one can even say quite a lot about Perfect Effort and Perfect Awareness; but when we come to Perfect Samadhi there would seem to be much less to say. It may well be that having said a little I will have to take refuge in silence. If this happens it should be taken as emphasizing the importance of this stage of the Path, and not otherwise.

The word *samādhi*, which is the same in both Sanskrit and Pali, literally means the state of being firmly fixed or established. This is the primary signification of the term, and it can be understood in two rather distinct ways. Firstly it can be understood as representing the fixation or establishment of the mind on a single object, which is *samādhi* in the sense of mental concentration. Secondly, and going much further, it can be understood as representing the fixation or establishment, not just of the mind, but of the whole being in a certain mode of consciousness or awareness. This is *samādhi* in the sense of Enlightenment or Buddhahood.

In the Theravada texts, or the texts of the Pali Canon, the word *samādhi* is usually understood in the first sense, as concentration or one-pointedness of mind. But in the Mahāyāna sutras the word *samādhi* is often used in the second sense, in the sense of being fixed or established in Ultimate Reality; in which case the word that is used instead of *samādhi* to denote one-pointedness of mind is generally *śamathā*, the precise meaning of which will be explained later.

This distinction between *samādhi* in the sense of concentration of mind in meditation, and *samādhi* in the sense of establishment of the whole being in Enlightenment, is vitally important. If Perfect Samadhi is taken as meaning merely good concentration, then the whole significance of this stage—and therewith the whole significance of the Noble Eightfold Path itself—becomes seriously distorted. Unfortunately this is often done: Perfect Samadhi is rendered as Right Concentration, and the impression is given that the whole of the spiritual path, the whole practical teaching of the Buddha as represented by the Noble Eightfold Path, culminates simply in concentration—the sort of thing you achieve in your meditation class almost every week.

One might indeed go further and say that in modern times each and every step of the Eightfold Path has been seriously undervalued, even minimized, with a very narrow and limited interpretation being given. This is unfortunate, because it makes the Noble Eightfold Path appear as something rather unattractive, rather confined, and it causes people to wonder how the Eightfold Path can be considered the central theme of the Buddha's whole teaching. To appreciate the significance of the Noble Eightfold Path we need an understanding of the significance of each stage, and I hope that in this present exposition I have been able to show that there is much more to the Eightfold Path than some of its modern exponents generally suspect.

Perfect Samadhi—the culminating phase of the Eightfold Path—is much more than just good concentration. Essentially Perfect Samadhi represents the fruition of the whole Path of Transformation. It represents the state of being fully and perfectly transformed, on all levels and in every aspect of one's being. In other words it represents the culmination of the process of transformation from an

unenlightened to an Enlightened state, and the complete
and perfect permeation of all aspects of one's being by that
Perfect Vision with which one started.

Perfect Samadhi means that Perfect Vision has in the
end triumphed, and now reigns supreme at every level of
one's being and consciousness. If Perfect Samadhi is understood in this way, then real sense is made of the Noble
Eightfold Path, and of one's pilgrimage along that Path.

Śamathā, Samāpatti, and *Samādhi*

Although *samādhi* in the sense of concentration and
samādhi in the sense of Enlightenment are quite distinct
and not to be confused, it is important to understand that
they are not mutually exclusive. Perhaps we would not be
going far wrong if we described them as the lower and
higher degrees of the same experience. One could also say
that between *samādhi* as concentration and *samādhi* as
Enlightenment there is an intermediate stage or degree
which is known in the Mahāyāna texts as *samāpatti*.
Samāpatti literally means attainments, and it suggests all
those spiritual experiences which, occurring as a result of
the practice of concentration, nevertheless fall short of
samādhi in the fullest sense. Thus we have three terms:
Śamathā (Pali *samatha*) or concentration, *samāpatti* or attainments, and *samādhi* in the full and final sense of Enlightenment itself. These three terms represent a single
progressive series of spiritual experiences, each introduc-
ing the next and preparing the way for it. By studying each
in turn we shall gain, as it were cumulatively, an idea or a
glimpse of the nature of *samādhi* in the more ultimate
sense.

Śamathā

Śamathā literally means tranquillity, though it is also sometimes translated as pacification, or calming down, or even

simply as calm. If we were to translate it as peace we probably would not be far wrong, because it is a state of profound peace and calm of mind, and even of the whole being. Mental activity in the sense of discursive thought or the clattering of the mental machinery is either minimal —that is, very subtle—or entirely absent. *Samathā* is also a state of perfect concentration or one-pointedness of mind, a state of integration of all the forces and energies of one's psycho-physical being. Thus *śamathā* corresponds to what are known as the four *dhyānas*, the four states or stages of higher consciousness which were discussed under the heading of Perfect Effort.

Śamathā is often divided into three degrees or levels or grades: concentration on a gross material object; concentration on a subtle counterpart of the gross object; and absorption into the subtle counterpart of the gross object. Since this may not be very clear, let me give a concrete illustration. Suppose you take up the practice of concentration on an image or picture of the Buddha. The image or picture is your gross object. You sit down in front of it and look at it—not staring, but just looking. You look at it without paying attention to anything else. You shut out all other sights, all other sense-impressions, and with eyes wide open you remain fully concentrated on that image or picture, taking it in fully and completely and being aware of nothing else.

In the second stage you close your eyes and see the image or picture of the Buddha just as clearly as if you had your eyes open and were looking at the material image or picture itself. This of course takes quite a bit of practice, and comes more easily to some than to others. The image you see vividly when your eyes are closed is the subtle, mental counterpart of the original material image or picture, and you concentrate on that. Eventually there is no sensory perception: you are completely concentrated on this mental—even archetypal—image or picture within.

In the third stage you continue concentrating, even more intensely and one-pointedly, on the subtle counterpart of the original gross image. As you concentrate on it you become, as it were, assimilated into it, absorbed in it. The distinction between the subject and the object eventually disappears, and you merge with the object of your concentration, and become identified with it.

I have taken concentration on an image or picture of the Buddha as an example of the practice of *samatha*, because here the difference between the degrees can be seen clearly; but in every type of concentration exercise we start by taking a gross object, work our way up to the subtle object, and then become absorbed in the subtle object, thus experiencing the three degrees, levels, or grades of *samatha* or tranquillity.

Samāpatti

Samāpatti literally means attainments, or experiences gained as a result of practising concentration. All those who practise concentration and meditation eventually get experiences of one kind or another. The type and degree of the experiences depends very much on personal temperament, and is not necessarily related to the degree of spiritual development. Sometimes people assume that if you have a lot of experiences of this sort you are more advanced than if you only have one or two or none at all; but it is not as simple as that.

The commonest sort of experience of an elementary nature is probably the experience of light. As the mind becomes more concentrated, you may see lights of various kinds—usually a white or yellowish light, sometimes bluish, and occasionally red or green, though these are comparatively rare. Experiences of this sort are an indication that the mind has become concentrated, that the level of awareness has been raised slightly, and that one has begun to contact something which is just a little bit beyond the ordinary conscious mind. Some people, instead of seeing lights, hear sounds. They may hear a very deep, sustained musical note, rather like a mantra, or they may even hear words pronounced, as it were, within themselves. They may hear these words very clearly at times, as though a voice is speaking to them. People who believe in God often think, of course, that it is God speaking to them, but according to Buddhist teaching these sounds or voices all come from the depths—and sometimes not even from the deepest depths—of one's own mind or consciousness.

Occasionally it also happens that in the course of their practice of concentration people have the experience of perceiving various scents. Sometimes it is as though the room in which they are sitting is pervaded by a sweet-smelling scent like that of jasmine or roses, and sometimes this scent can even be smelt by other people. This too is a sign that the mind is becoming more subtle, more refined and rarified, and that one is contacting a higher level of consciousness.

As one progresses the experiences change. I am not going to try to give you an account of all the different experiences one may have, but I will mention just a few more of the typical ones which are likely to occur with most people. One may have the experience of suddenly seeing landscapes of various kinds unfolding before one, some with hills and trees and stretching, sometimes, as though for miles. One may see brilliant blue sky or flashing geometrical patterns, or patterns made as though of jewels, or mandala-like forms and figures. One may also see other forms of various kinds, such as faces or eyes. All these experiences are quite common in the case of people who practise concentration and meditation even to a slight extent. One may also experience something a little different, such as a change in one's body weight: one may feel very heavy, as though one could not possibly get up; or one may feel very light, as though one was going to float away like thistledown. There may be experiences of intense heat or cold, and sometimes these changes of temperature can be perceived by other people.

Some people who keep up the practice of concentration and meditation over a long period—though not all, because this is a matter of temperament—find that not only do their minds become highly sensitized, but that they develop various subtle senses. They may become aware that they are understanding what other people are thinking, or they may develop the faculties which we in the West call clairvoyance and clairaudience. According to Buddhist teaching—in fact according to Buddhist *experience*—these faculties develop as the result of practising concentration and meditation, when the whole being becomes more refined and subtle. But I must emphasize again that they do not develop in the case of everybody. Some people apparently can even go the whole way— even realize Nirvana—without developing any of these faculties at all.

Other *samāpatti* experiences include, perhaps more importantly, the experience of intense joy, bliss, and ecstacy, and of an ineffable peace descending upon one and enfolding one. This occurs especially at the time of meditation, but it can occur at other times also. Even more important—and here *samāpatti* begins to merge into *samā dhi*—you may attain flashes of insight. It is as though a veil had been suddenly rent and, just for an instant, you see things as they are—and then the veil closes. But you do get a glimpse, or a flash. You might suddenly comprehend the truth of a teaching you had known for a long time, but had never realized or had any insight into—something you had read about in books, and thought you knew very well. When you have this flash of insight into that truth, that reality, you realize that before you did not know it at all—not one little bit. It is not that you understood it partially or fairly well—not that at all. When you really *see*, in an actual flash of insight, you realize that when you knew this truth only from books or from hearsay you did not really know it *at all*.

All the experiences I have described are *samāpatti* experiences, and as we have seen there is an immense variety of them. No one person experiences them all, but all those who tread the path of concentration and meditation experience some of them at least.

Samādhi

I have already said that *samādhi* proper is the state of being established in Reality, or of being Enlightened. There are many ways of looking at this state. Often it is described in negative terms, for instance in terms of the destruction of the *āsravas*. The word *āsrava* (Pali *āsava*) means a poisonous flux, a bias, a lop-sidedness in our nature. The *āsravas* are three in number. Firstly there is the *kāmāsrava* (Pali *kāmāsava*), the bias towards, or the poisonous flux of, the desire or craving for sense experience for its own sake, on its own level. Secondly there is *bhavāsrava* (Pali *bhavāsava*), or the bias towards, the poisonous flux of, conditioned existence—in other words the attachment to or desire for any mode of existence short of Enlightenment itself. Thirdly there is *āvidyāsrava* (Pali *avijjāsava*), the bias towards or the poisonous flux of ignorance, in the sense of spiritual darkness and unawareness. Thus in negative terms *samādhi* proper is described as the complete absence of these three poisonous fluxes or biases. It is a state in which sense experiences and material things mean nothing: a state in which there is no desire for any kind of conditioned existence, no real interest in anything other than Nirvana or Enlightenment, and no shadow of ignorance or spiritual darkness.

In addition to this negative description of *samādhi* there are various positive descriptions—though here we must tread warily, and understand that we are trying to give a hint or two about something which it is far beyond the power of words to express. Some of the texts mention a group of three *samādhis*, in the higher sense of the term. This does not mean that these are three mutually exclusive states—the so-called three *samādhis* are more like different aspects or dimensions of the one *samādhi*.

1. The Imageless Samadhi

The first of these three *samādhis* is known as the Imageless (Pali and Skt *animitta*). It indicates the perfect freedom of the state of *samādhi* from all thoughts, all conceptualization. If we can imagine a state in which we are fully and clearly conscious, fully and clearly aware at the highest possible level, without any discursive thought—if we imagine the mind as being like a beautiful, bright blue, clear sky, without even a speck of cloud—this is what the experience of the Imageless Samadhi would be like. Usually the sky of the mind is full of clouds: grey clouds, black clouds, sometimes even storm clouds; but occasionally clouds tinged with gold. The state of *samādhi* is a state free from *all* clouds of thought, *all* conceptualization.

2. The Directionless Samadhi

The second *samādhi*—or aspect or dimension of *samādhi*—is known as the Directionless or the Unbiased (Skt *apraṇihita*, Pali *appaṇihita*). The Directionless Samadhi is a state in which there is no particular direction in which one wants to go, there is no preference. One just remains poised, like a sphere resting on a completely horizontal plane, with no reason why of its own accord it should roll in any particular direction. The Enlightened mind—the mind established in *samādhi*—is like this. It has no tendency or inclination to any one direction because it has no individual or egotistic desire. This is a difficult state to describe, but perhaps if one thinks in terms of a perfect spontaneity, without any urge or impulse to do anything in particular, one may get somewhere near it.

3. *The Samadhi of the Voidness*

The third aspect or dimension of *samādhi* is known as the Samadhi of the Voidness, or *śūnyatā* (Pali *suññatā*). *Śūnyatā* does not mean emptiness or voidness in the literal sense. It means Reality. *Śūnyatā-samādhi* is the state of full and complete realization of the ultimate nature of existence, which cannot be put into words. It is not just a glimpse, as in the stage of Perfect Vision, but a full, total, and perfect realization. This Samadhi of the Voidness is connected in some texts with the *ekalakṣaṇa-samādhi* or Samadhi of One Characteristic, also known as the Samadhi of Same- or Even-Mindedness. This is an experience where one sees everything as having the same characteristics. We normally see some things as good, some as bad. Some things we regard as pleasant, some as unpleasant. Some things we like, some we dislike; some are near, some are far; some are past, some are present, and some are future. In this way we assign different characteristics to things. But in the Samadhi of the Voidness you see everything as having the same characteristic: it is all *śūnyatā*, all ultimately real, and in its ultimate depths all *the same*. Inasmuch as everything is basically the same, there is no reason why one should have different attitudes towards different things; one has the same attitude towards everything, and enjoys, therefore, a state of peace, tranquillity, stability, and rest.

Those of you who are interested in Zen, especially in Hui Neng and his *Platform Scripture* (also known as *The Sutra of Hui Neng*), may be interested to know that both the

Samadhi of One Characteristic and the Samadhi of Even-Mindedness are mentioned in the *Platform Scripture*. This brings us to a very important point in connection with Zen Buddhism. Hui Neng, you may remember, says that *samādhi* and *prajñā* (or Wisdom) are not different, but in reality the same thing. He says that *samādhi* is the quintessence of *prajñā*, and *prajñā* the function of *samādhi*, and he illustrates this by saying that *samādhi* is like a lamp, and *prajñā* or Wisdom like the light of the lamp.

This identity, or at least non-duality, of *samādhi* and *prajñā*, is a very important teaching of Hui Neng and of the Zen school generally, and some Western students of Zen have found it difficult and confusing. Sometimes they have even distorted it. The reason for this is that they take the word *samādhi* to mean concentration, and think that Hui Neng is equating this with Wisdom, making nonsense of his teaching and leading people far astray indeed. The *samādhi* of Hui Neng, however, in this passage at least, is *samādhi* in the highest sense: *samādhi* as identical with the eighth step of the Noble Eightfold Path, as we have explained it. In other words *samādhi* in this passage means the state of being fully established in the Enlightened mode of being. This is in fact quite clear from the *Platform Sutra*. Hui Neng says quite clearly and emphatically in the sutra that people misinterpret the 'Samadhi of One Characteristic', thinking that it means sitting quietly and continuously without letting any ideas arise in the mind. In other words they think it means concentration—an interpretation Hui Neng rejects. If it were just concentration it would make us like inanimate objects. *Samādhi* in the real sense, he says—in his sense, in the Ch'an or Zen sense—is something quite different.

This does not mean that Hui Neng is against sitting in meditation, or against concentrating the mind. He is only saying that concentration, or *śamathā*, is not *samādhi* in the fullest and highest sense, or in the *real* sense. Concentration is just concentration: it is not that *samādhi* which, according to his teaching, is identical with *prajñā*. True *samādhi*, Hui Neng says, remains the same under all circumstances and conditions. It is not something you experience only when you sit and meditate.

In Zen monasteries and temples the three stages of *śamathā*, *samāpatti*, and *samādhi*—in the highest sense—are all taught and practised; but Zen shares the first two with the other schools of Buddhism. The specific contribution of Zen lies in its teaching about *samādhi* in the ultimate sense, in the sense of the state of being established in the Enlightened mode of being, and especially in its teaching about the non-duality of *samādhi* and *prajñā*.

The Noble Eightfold Path as a Cumulative Process
We are now in a better position to understand what it is that we are trying to attain when we follow the Buddha's Noble Eightfold Path. We are trying to attain a higher mode of being and consciousness. We are not just trying to achieve 'Right Concentration'. What we are aiming at is a total transformation of our whole being, at every level and in all its aspects, in the light of the initial Perfect Vision. And, so far as we can see, this step or stage of Perfect Samadhi marks the culmination of the whole evolutionary process—at least, the whole process of the Higher Evolution.

At this point I should add a word of warning, or at least of explanation. The Noble Eightfold Path is, as its name tells us, a path or way (Skt *mārga*, Pali *magga*) made up of eight steps or stages, and the Buddhist spiritual life consists of following this path. This is familiar imagery, which we use all the time in Buddhism, but we should beware of interpreting too literally what is essentially a figure of speech. We are so easily misled by words—so easily take them at face value. It is true that in a way the spiritual life does consist in following a path, going from one stage to the next. But in another way the spiritual life is not at all like following a path. When we go along a path we leave the earlier stages behind. They are finished and done with. But in the case of the spiritual path it is not like that. The spiritual path is a cumulative process, like rolling a snowball along the ground—it grows and expands all the time. It is not that first we have Perfect Vision, and then when Perfect Vision is finished and done with we forget all about it and go on to Perfect Emotion, and so on. It is not like that at all, though understandably we think in those terms. The spiritual path is in fact a *cumulative* process, a process of growth or expansion, and in a sense we are following all the stages of the Eightfold Path all the time.

How is this? Suppose that, just for an instant, we experience Perfect Vision. It may be while we are meditating, or out walking in the countryside, or listening to music, or even as we pause in the midst of the traffic. Howsoever it may be, we have an experience of Perfect Vision. Something opens up within us and, for a fraction of a second, we see things as they really are. For a fraction of a second we are in contact with something Ultimate—even with Reality. But then what happens? This moment of Perfect Vision influences our emotions and, to some extent at least, we develop Perfect Emotion, the second step of the Path. It also overflows into our speech and influences that, so that our speech becomes more like Perfect Speech. Our actions are also influenced, at least subtly and indirectly. We are changed in all these ways, and so it goes on. At some other time—maybe weeks, months, or years later— there is another moment of Perfect Vision, and the whole process repeats itself. We are influenced still more by Perfect Vision, our emotions become more like Perfect Emotion, our speech become more like Perfect Speech, and so the process continues.

At the very beginning of these lectures I pointed out that *anga* means limb, not step or stage, so that the *ārya-aṣṭāṅgika-mārga* (Pali *ariya-aṭṭhāṅgika-magga*) is the eight-limbed, or eight-membered, or eight-shooted path, not the path of eight successive discrete steps or stages. Thus the spiritual life is more like a process of growth, more like the unfolding of a living thing, than it is like someone going from one stage to the next of a path, or from one rung to the next of a ladder.

Spiritual growth is like the development of a tree. First you have a sapling rooted in the earth, and then one day the rain falls, perhaps quite heavily. The rain is absorbed through the roots of the sapling, the sap rises and spreads into the branches and twigs—and the tree grows. There is a pause, and then again the rain falls, again the sap rises, and this time not only does it spread into the branches and twigs, but leaves begin to unfold. If no rain falls for a time the tree may wither a little, but eventually more rain comes—there may even be a real cloudburst, a downpour —and then not only does the sap rise into the branches and twigs and leaves, but flowers begin to unfold. The following of the Eightfold Path is like that. First there is a spiritual experience, a glimpse of Reality, or in other words a moment of Perfect Vision. This is like the falling of the rain. And just as the sap rises and spreads into the branches and twigs, so Perfect Vision gradually transforms the different aspects of our being. Emotion is transformed, speech is transformed, actions and livelihood are transformed— even volitions and awareness are transformed. As a result of that moment of Perfect Vision, to some extent the whole being is transformed.

This process is repeated over and over again, at ever higher levels, until at last the entire being is completely transformed, and nothing is left unchanged. One is entirely pervaded by the light of Enlightenment. *This* is the stage of Perfect Samadhi—the stage when one's whole being and consciousness, having been brought into line with one's original Perfect Vision, has been thoroughly transformed and transmuted, from the lowest up to the highest levels. It is also, of course, the state of Enlightenment or Buddhahood. The Path has now been completely fulfilled—has, in fact, become the Goal—and the whole process of the Higher Evolution has been perfected.

With this we come to the end of our journey. At least we come to the end of that journey in our imagination. It is my hope that this imaginary journey of ours, on which we have had the company of so many people, has been of some use both to those who have been trying to follow the Path for some time, and to those who are newcomers to the study and practice of the Buddha's teaching, and that it will help them follow the Buddha's Noble Eightfold Path, not just in imagination, but in reality.

Index

Index

Also from Windhorse Publications

A Guide to the Buddhist Path
Sangharakshita

No matter how enticing the Buddhist path may seem, the modern Westerner will surely hesitate before setting foot upon it. So many schools have evolved over the centuries, so much literature has emerged, and so many people have left their mark on the tradition, that it can be hard even to know what Buddhism actually is. Which teachings really matter? How does one begin to practise Buddhism in a systematic way? This is confusing territory. Without a guide one can easily get dispirited or lost.

In this highly readable anthology a leading Western Buddhist sorts out fact from myth, essence from cultural accident, to reveal the fundamental ideals and teachings of Buddhism. The result is a reliable map of the Buddhist path that anyone can follow. It is just the guide we need.

Sangharakshita is an ideal companion on the path. He is intimately familiar with the various strands of the Buddhist tradition and profoundly experienced in Buddhist practice. As founder of a major Western Buddhist movement he has helped thousands of people to make an effective contact with the richness and beauty of the Buddha's teachings.

256 pages, index, bibliography, illustrated
Paperback, £10.95
ISBN 0-904766-35-7

For a complete catalogue of Windhorse books, please write to Windhorse Publications, 136 Renfield Street, Glasgow, G2 3AU, Scotland